Nā Mele Hula

Volume 2

Hawaiian Hula Rituals and Chants

Emma Lani

1. A Kilohana o Kalani
   Nana ia Hanalei
   O ke one o Mahamoku
   Me ka wai o Lumahai

2. O ka lae hala o Naue
   Alai ia e ka noe
   O Maunahina ko lalo
   O ke alanui kui lima

3. Ui ae nei Emma Lani
   E huli hoi kakou
   Ma ke alanui Ohia
   Ala kipapa a ola

4. O ke anakoo kai luna
   Naele o Alakai la
   O Kulou o Emmalani
   I ke anu o Aipo

5. Uhi paa mai e ka noe
   Halana mai aka wai
   Puili lala i ke ahi
   I kapa no ia uka

6. O ka leo ka mea aloha
   I ka heahea ana mai
   Pehea mai oukou
   Maanei ma Kamehana

7. Ka ihona o Kanahele
   A hiki i ka wai kai
   He piina ikiiki ia
   A kukala a ka manu

8. Hoomaha aku o Kalani
   I ka lehua makanoe
   He lehua lei apiki
   Pauku me ka pai niu

9. He paia ala i ke anu
   He nohea i ka waonahele
   Kupaoa i ke ala
   Ke ala o ka hinahina

Helen Desha Beamer, grandmother of Nona Beamer, recorded many of her family's traditional chants as well as her own compositions on the reverse sides of her husband's business ledger, begun in 1897. (Transcription of this chant appears on pp. 68–69.)

Nā Mele Hula

Volume 2
Hawaiian Hula Rituals and Chants

Compiled and Annotated
by
Nona Beamer

Edited by
Mauliola Cook and S. Kaliko Beamer Trapp

Illustrated by Roy Hewetson

Hawaiian Language Consultants
Pōhaku Nishimitsu
S. Kaliko Beamer Trapp
Mauliola Cook

The Institute for Polynesian Studies
Brigham Young University-Hawai'i Campus
Lā'ie, Hawai'i

Text copyright © 2001 by Nona Beamer
Illustrations copyright © 2001 by The Institute for Polynesian Studies
All Rights Reserved
Manufactured in the United States of America

Library of Congress Control Number 87-751437
ISBN 0-939154-55-2 (pbk.)
ISBN 0-939154-57-9 (pbk. & cassette tape)

This book is printed on acid-free paper and meets the guidelines for
permanence and durability of the Council on Library Resources

Published by:
The Institute for Polynesian Studies
BYUH Box 1979
55-220 Kulanui Street
Lāʻie, Hawaiʻi 96762-1294

Distributed for The Institute for Polynesian Studies
by the University of Hawaiʻi Press:

Order Department
University of Hawaiʻi Press
2840 Kolowalu Street
Honolulu, Hawaiʻi 96822
ph. 1-888-UHPRESS • fax 1-800-650-7811
www.hawaii.edu/uhpress • e-mail uhpbooks@hawaii.edu

To
My Dear Sons
Keola and Kapono Beamer

who continue to add immeasurable joy and love to my life.
From them I have learned more about respect and humility.

I dedicate this volume to them in appreciation.

"May all good be with you
E pōmaikaʻi ʻolua

To fill your hearts with love"
A e piha hoʻi i ke aloha

CHRIS MCLUCKIE

CONTENTS

ix
PREFACE

xi
ACKNOWLEDGMENTS

1
INTRODUCTION

PART I: NĀ HANA HOʻOHANOHANO (RITUALS AND CEREMONIES)

Nā Mele Oli No Laka
Chants for Laka

15
Malu Ke Ala
The Path Is Cleared

16
Pule No Ke Akua ʻO Laka
Prayer to the Goddess Laka

17
Eia Au E Laka
Here I Am O Laka

18–19
Kānaenae No Laka
A Prayer Chant for Laka

20
Pule Kuahu
Altar Prayer

21
Pule Hoʻonoa
A Prayer to Lift Sacred Restrictions

Nā Mele Oli No Ka Hoʻomākaukau ʻAna
Chants in Preparation for Hula

24
Kūnihi Ka Mauna
The Mountain Stands Steep

25
Oli Aloha
Chant of Loving Welcome

26
Aloha Nā Hale
Beloved Are the Houses

27
Eia Hawaiʻi
Behold Hawaiʻi

28
Hālau Waiʻanae
Waiʻanae Longhouse

29
Oli Kūpeʻe
Chant for Wristlets and Anklets

30
Oli Pāʻū
Skirt Chant

31
Oli Lei
Lei Chant

PART II: NĀ MELE HULA (DANCE CHANTS)

Pele
The Fire Goddess

36
Hoʻopuka Ē Ka Lā I Kai O Unulau
The Sun Rises over the Sea of Unulau

37
ʻO Ke Mele Mua Kēia O Ka Hula Pele
The First Chant of the Pele Dances

38–39
Puʻuʻoniʻoni
Tremble Hill

40-41
Ke Pohā Nei
It Is Rustling

42-43
'Oaka Ē Ka Lani
The Heavens Flash

Nā Ali'i
The Chiefs

46-47
E Manono
O Manono

48-49
Moe Aku
Asleep [Are We]

50-51
He Wahine Holo Lio
A Horsewoman

52-53
Kau Ī Lua
Doubly Chilled

54-55
Aia I Haili Kō Lei Nani
There at Haili Is Your Precious Garland

56-57
I Aloha I Kō A Ka Wai
How Loving When Pulled by the Current

58-59
Lanakila
Victory

60
No Ke Ano Ahiahi
In the Evening Time

61
He Ma'i No Kalani
A Personal Chant for the Chief

62-63
He Ma'i No 'Iolani
A Personal Chant for 'Iolani

Nā Wahi Pana
Historic and Legendary Places

66-67
'Au'a 'Ia E Kama Ē Kona Moku
Child Hold on to Your Land

68-69
A Kilohana 'O Kalani
The Chiefess Went to Kilohana

70-71
'Ike I Ke One Kani A'o Nohili
See the Barking Sands of Nohili

72
E Ho'i Ke Aloha I Ni'ihau
Love Returns to Ni'ihau

73
He Moku Ka'ula
The Island of Ka'ula

74
A Puna Au
I Was in Puna

75
APPENDIX

76
BIBLIOGRAPHY

77-81
INDEX

82
INDEX TO FIRST LINES

PREFACE TO VOLUME 2

I am proud and happy to share these chants in this second volume of *Nā Mele Hula* on behalf of myself and my family, all of whom I "treasure beyond measure."

Not a day goes by without thoughts of my dear parents, Louise Leiomalama and Pono Beamer, formerly of Waimea, Hawai'i. Since I began working on this volume my dear father, rancher and Hawaiian extraordinaire, and my dear mother have passed away. I have left their presence in this volume as I originally wrote it. These are such poignant memories, of sitting with my parents at 'Imiola Church kissing my dear Mother's sweet hands and face, hugging Papa while his strong baritone voice was happily harmonizing the Hawaiian congregational hymns—and always my heart overflows with love for them and tears of joy stream down my face. Overwhelming love for my dear parents saturates my life fully, for they are my wellspring from which all goodness flows.

We speak of Sweetheart Grandma often, Helen Desha Beamer, Papa's mother. She is the "psychic link," as my son Keola says, that fuses our family together. The love gets stronger from one generation to the next—from Great Grandma, Isabella Ka'ili Desha, on down to grandson Kamana, Kapono's son. The love has strengthened, as we each add our spirit to the family calabash of chants and songs. Sons Keola and Kapono are still expanding their Hawai'iana in many directions, and my pride and joy increases daily with their many accomplishments.

How lucky we are to have their extraordinary talent in our family bank. It adds lustre to our lives and helps to fill our hearts. When I see the Hawai'iana enrichment my family has added to my sons' lives, I am indebted to all of them for the love extended in so many ways . . . often unknown to them as they give so generously. At a family wedding of brother Keola's son, Lono, I was filled with added love and admiration for the family. Brother Keola and wife Cotieng dancing *kahiko* (traditional *hula*) and singing, cousin Mahi with his piano genius, and he and Robert Cazimero singing so gloriously. There was sister-in-law Myrtle Kau'inohea, brother Pono's wife, the outstanding dancer of the family, and cousins Marmionette Ka'aihue, Gaye Beamer, and Lei Desha Becker Furtado, also *hula* masters. How can we be so blessed? I think the blessings are multiplied because we all share our Hawai'iana so willingly, with warm *aloha*. In my heart, I feel that the next generation is secure in their love and in their lives. Now my concern is for the *mo'opuna* (grandchildren). How can I add Hawai'iana enrichment to grandson Kamana's life? First, isn't the priority love? Speak of any enrichment and it must be love! Speak of Hawai'iana and it must be love of your Hawaiian self and the Hawaiian culture.

Aloha continues to be real today. Perhaps, though, the reality of love needs to be expressed more, daily, in everything we do. The basic premise of *aloha* is universal. It is kindness, caring and sharing good things. In our family we have used this poetic saying. This loving thought is very sustaining to us. It fills us with good feelings and we feel honored to share love: *"E pōmaika'i 'oukou a e piha ho'i i ke aloha"* (May all good be with you [all] to fill your hearts with love).

The foundation of the Hawaiian culture is the language. Hawaiian chant and dance are our vital links that strengthen the bonds of our heritage. As we share these chants in this second volume, I write of my personal feelings and experiences with each chant.

Nāpua Stevens Poire was a teacher, lecturer, Hawai'iana expert and a very special friend. She was a member of our early Hilo classes with Sweetheart Grandma and over the years we shared loving memories. I asked her if I could interview her for this book. She was gracious, as always, and we spent a lovely morning together at her Kāne'ohe, O'ahu, home. When she died in January 1990, I read and reread my interview notes. Nāpua exuded so much love for us all and especially for Sweetheart Grandma. When she spoke of Grandma, her eyes misted and her voice warmed. Nāpua was one of the older girls in our *hula* classes at Halehuki, Grandma's lovely house on the banks of the Wailuku River. Her words are so precious. I am honored to include them here. "The charm and quality of Aunty Helen's teachings are with me to this day," Nāpua told me. "She taught me so much more than just the dance. It was a complete living philosophy that I hold dear to my heart."

My dear mother, Louise Leiomalama, was also in the class, standing in the third line. I was constantly looking over my shoulder for her smile of approval, until Great Grandma would scold, "Tcha! *Keu nō ho'i mū li'ili'i. Kū nō 'oe i ka pāpā i kona wā 'u'uku.*" She was saying, "Goodness sake! You little rascal, you are just like your papa, ha-ha, when he was young" or something like that. If she had said it in English, calling me a *mū li'ili'i*, little insect, I would have run out of the room with loud sobbing.

Hawaiian philosophy is as important for teachers and students as is the research and background of who, where and why. I was tempted to repeat important information that appears in the first volume; however, I decided to assume that you the reader have already read it. The tape accompanying this volume, as well as the one accompanying Volume 1, is an important learning tool. Do bear in mind that the text material is foremost. Be honest in your heart and mind and give yourself the luxury and pleasure of understanding. Your confidence in using the material will reflect your honesty and joy.

At this time I would like to apologize for errors and omissions made in the very first printing of Volume 1; they were corrected in all subsequent printings: p. 10, the chant "Ka Liko Pua Kukui" is in honor of Moloka'i, whose island flower is the *kukui—E kala mai e kō Moloka'i* (Our apologies to Moloka'i); p. 28, Princess Likelike was the second, not the first, of her family to die—her brother, William Pitt Leleiōhoku, died before her, in 1877; p. 30, the Republic of Hawai'i was established, without a popular vote, in 1894 and annexation to the United States was in 1898; p. 72, add *hula* type *hula pū'ili* (bamboo rattle).

With completion of this Volume 2, my thoughts are now turned to Volume 3. My dear friend Mauli Cook, my dear young *hānai* son, Kaliko Beamer Trapp, and I are already planning to have contemporary Hawaiian chants as the focus of our next efforts. I have some special students and young friends in mind to share some of their original chant compositions. I can hardly wait to start the new work and encourage our young generation to be creative. Write new chants and inspire us!

Mahalo for helping our Beamer Family Hawaiian Culture Scholarships by purchasing this volume. May you enjoy success in your work with love in your hearts. I wish you happy Hawai'iana.

Love to all of you,
Aunty Nona Beamer
Pulelehua, Puna, Hawai'i

ACKNOWLEDGMENTS

Pōhaku Nishimitsu was an invaluable contributor to this volume. His deep knowledge of historical and geographical aspects of Hawaiian culture provided us with otherwise elusive references and translations. As he is a *kumu hula* schooled in traditions that differ from mine, our chant variations became apparent as we worked together.

Following the Hawaiian style of passing on *hula* knowledge I acknowledge and honor my family traditions, at the same time being grateful for the enrichment shared with me by others. We must always remember the classic *'ōlelo no'eau* (wise saying), *"A'ole i pau ka 'ike i ka hālau ho'okahi"* (All wisdom is not taught in your school. One learns from many schools). This philosophy has shaped my work and my life. It behooves us to practice this philosophy more lovingly today.

The late Dr. Donald Kilolani Mitchell and Mr. Frank Midkiff were always my Hawai'iana champions, since 1935 when I entered Kamehameha School for Girls at age twelve. Their passing is here noted and their love and belief in me continues to enrich my life.

We are indebted to Mary Kawena Pūku'i and Ka'upena Wong for their invaluable contributions to the Hawaiian culture. Ka'upena continues to be one of my favorite "cousins"! Mandy Bowers and Sigrid Southworth of the Hawai'iana Library of the Kamehameha Schools have been a joyful resource team. I have called upon them innumerable times over the past years. They have always been exceptionally kind and loving to me.

I wish also to extend my thanks to Betty Tatar of the Bishop Museum staff and Marguerite Ashford of the Punahou School Library for their kind encouragement.

Adelaide Suits, Phyllis and John Ohanian, and my *hula* sisters Betty Beck, Geri Sasabe, Alyce Ikeoka, Barbara Goodman, Dorothy Fonte and Susan Rose have all encouraged me to pursue this work.

Mona Cameron began working with me when we lived on O'ahu. Now that our paths have led us both to live in the peaceful forests of Puna, she continues to be a joyful addition to my life and a wonderful help in my work. A similar parallel exists with my friend Chris McLuckie. She has also made the move from O'ahu to the island of Hawai'i and I am happy to include her photographic work of my sons in the Dedication. Vivian Ontai has worked long hours on the computer. My dear Mauliola Cook is a constant love in my life. Her patience with me is endearing and it endures. I am grateful for the inspiration that she has put in my heart.

My dear friend Bette Bright, my sweet Mother and Papa, my dear sons Keola and Kapono, and my grandson Kamana have all given my life extraordinary depth of spirit. Family members mother Louise Leiomalama, brother C. Keola Beamer, son Kapono Beamer and grandson Kamana Beamer have added their voices to the tape accompanying this volume. How lucky we are to have them!

Kaliko Beamer Trapp has added a sparkle and a deeper dimension to my life. My heart goes out to him: His constant willingness is enhanced by his deep love for Hawai'i and the cultures of Polynesia. I am indebted to him for his wonderful Hawaiian language expertise, which he shares so willingly.

My life continues to grow and be blessed by the

recent *hānai* of a dear daughter, Maile Kapuailohia Beamer Loo. She is a Stanford University graduate with a degree in artificial intelligence. Her Kamehameha Schools experience sparked her interest in Beamer-style *hula* and her Hālau Hula 'O Kaho'oilina Aloha is now in its fourth year. The Beamer style of teaching and dancing is flourishing. I am proud and grateful.

To add more joy to our work, Maile and dear friend Kēhau Castro organized the nonprofit Hula Preservation Society to perpetuate the cultural knowledge of the *kūpuna*, so generations yet to come can hear the wisdom in their voices and know their unique spirit. For the past two years Maile and I have been documenting ancient *hula* types through participation in the State Foundation on Culture and the Arts' Folk Arts Program.

Thank you dear reader. Your purchase of this book and tape continues to benefit our seven Beamer Family Hawaiian Culture Scholarships at the Kamehameha Schools. Mahalo. I love you all.

Nā Mele Hula

Volume 2

Hawaiian Hula Rituals and Chants

INTRODUCTION

Chant and *Hula* Types

The chant types and styles and *hula* types used to describe each *mele* (chant) are those taught to us in our family. They do not reflect any "across the board" or "locked in" classifications. In our family, a *mele* is a poem to be chanted. Therefore, a *mele hula* is a chanted poem accompanied by dance. Generally speaking, an *oli* is nonmetered and less melodic than a *mele*. Also, an *oli* is usually not accompanied by *hula*. In our family, however, *oli* can be performed with formal gestures.

In this Volume 2, we have taken the advice of ethnomusicologist Betty Tatar of the Bishop Museum staff, who suggested musical notation for these chants is not necessary. Rather, we made the Volume 2 tape without accompaniment. We chanted the words and the rhythm. There is no instrumentation, for I wanted to keep the chant line as clear as I could so the listener could follow the voice and enhance his or her own style. I have always believed that notation is too restrictive, that teachers and students would follow the notes rigidly and not use their own expression. Traditional text and type are mandatory, but style gives each chanter a little leeway to be creative, especially in this present generation with so much great talent abounding.

Chant Heritage from My *Kūpuna Kuakahi* (Great-Grandparents)

One of my loving and endearing memories of my great-grandmother, Isabella Ka'ili Desha, was her sweet voice calling out a welcome chant as friends approached our home in Hilo. From the sidewalk near the Wailuku River bridge, there were six or eight coral steps surrounded by fern and *waiawī 'ula'ula* (strawberry guava). As friends reached the top step and began walking toward the house along wide stepping stones set in the green lawn, Great Grandma would call out a heartwarming welcome. Large mango trees shaded the front lawn and fragrant *laua'e* fern surrounded several *loulu* palms. These form a vivid picture in my mind, coupled with a deep stirring of love for Great Grandma. Her eyes would often fill with tears and her outstretched arms seemed so eager to embrace the friends. There were emotional greetings and voices raised in gentle wailing sounds, *"Auē, ka lō'ihi o ka hui 'ole o kākou e o'u hoa aloha ē"* (Alas, long time I have not set my eyes upon you, my friends). Before our classes Great Grandma would go out to sit in her *koa* wood rocker on the *lānai* (porch). She didn't chant for the *keiki* (children) that came scampering across the lawn, but it was so loving when she greeted one of her dear friends.

Another of my vivid recollections, the chanting voice of my great-grandfather, George Langhern Desha, comes drifting back into my mind every so often. He was our Hilo postmaster. I loved him in a passionate way, as children can be passionate and possessive! An indelible event occurred when we were at the Beamer volcano house, set back in a shady forest of *'ōhi'a lehua* trees on the *ma uka* (inland) side of the volcano road. The house made me laugh, for it was a funny-looking box on stilts, with a round, green wooden water tank topped with wire mesh sitting obtrusively and squat nearby. Great Grandpa and I were sitting on the *lānai*. He was telling me about our cousin Princess Elizabeth Kahanu, wife of Prince Kūhiō Kalaniana'ole. She visited us whenever she came to the Big Island, and she sat just where we were sitting. Great Grandpa said he had chanted for her, and I wanted to hear the chant. He uttered a strange, low guttural—an animal sound, like a dog growling. It was so unlike his natural voice. It was frightening to me, spooky and ghostly. The chant was "Ke Kānāwai 'O Māmalahoe" (The Law of the Splintered Paddle). Then he told me the story of Kamehameha 'Ekahi and his proclamation of this law on the island of Hawai'i. I have taught this as a *kākala* (rough, harsh chant style) just as I heard Great Grandpa chant it. I have never heard another chant like it.

Ke Kānāwai 'O Māmalahoe
The Law of the Splintered Paddle

E nā kānaka
E mālama 'oukou i ke akua,
A e mālama ho'i i ke kanaka nui a me ke kanaka iki;
E hele ka 'elemakule, ka luahine, a me ke kama
A moe i ke ala,
'A'ohe mea nāna e ho'opilikia,
Hewa nō, make!

O my people,
Honor thy god,
Respect alike [the rights of] men great and humble;
See to it that our aged, our women, and our children
Lie down to sleep by the roadside,
Without fear of harm.
Disobey, and die!

This decree was made at Kaipalaoa, Hilo, at Kahale'iole'ole (the House without Rats) sometime between 1796 and 1802. The law was spoken by Kamehameha I in memory of his steersman, who lost his life in a 1783 incident when a fisherman splintered a canoe paddle over the great *ali'i*'s head at Pāpa'i Bay, Puna (now called King's Landing). It was also a statement of forgiveness for the fisherman and his companion. This law guarantees the safety of the highways to all.

Instrumentation

The *ipu heke* (double gourd drum) is the chief instrument of accompaniment used with *mele hula* (dance chants). The *pahu* (sharkskin drum) is used for more serious, formal chants.

There are twenty-five Hawaiian instruments and implements used to tell *hula* stories. Following is a discussion of the six *hula ho'okani* (percussion dance) instruments most often used, with their respective rhythms. Each instrument has its own name, distinct sound, and playing pattern. From north to south, Kaua'i to the island of Hawai'i, the patterns differ. The amazing depth and variety in the *hula* become evident the more research we do. I talked to a Hawaiian *kupuna wahine* (female elder) on Moloka'i who recalled the *'ūlili* (triple or spinning gourd rattle) being used by Moloka'i dancers without the *ali'ipoe*[1] seeds filling the gourds. Thus the gourds were whirring but not rattling. What a unique *hula* style! This is known only on Moloka'i. Was that an accident, no dry seeds available? Or was it a purposeful omission? For what reason? My dear friend, the late Dr. Kilolani Mitchell, was with me when we were privileged to share this information. We were both puzzled. Perhaps a reader will shed light on this happenstance.

The term "instrument" has, for me, denoted that it was fashioned or handcrafted, whereas the term "implement" has connoted a natural piece such as wood or stone. As *keiki* we had great fun looking for guava branches for our *hula kālā'au* (dances with sticks). Pololū Valley, Waipio, Hawai'i, was the best place to gather *'ili'ili* (*hula* pebbles). In my adult years, my brother Towhead helped me gather *'ili'ili* there for my classes. At the mouth of the valley, where the ocean tide meets the mountain stream, the sound of the clattering pebbles was heavenly music—I have never heard another sound like it. I thought the *'ili'ili* "voices" were subtle and husky, very musical and haunting.

We have used the word *"waena"* (middle, between) to mean the rhythm section between verses. Modern terminology frequently uses the word "vamp" for the familiar musical pattern played between each verse. This may be acceptable for *hapa haole* (part-English) songs, but I find it better to use the word *"kāholo"* (vamp) to signify the "in-between" of *hula 'auana* (modern-style dance) and *"waena"* for *hula kahiko* (ancient dance). Often the terms *"ki'i pā"* (common motion—movement

---

1. Ornamental cannas *(Canna indica)* whose seeds are used for *lei* as well as rattles.

from side to side—used in *hula hoʻokani*) and "*waena*" are used interchangeably, but it is not so in our family. *Kiʻi pā* is the action of the instrument and *waena* is the between-verse section.

The first rule we were taught for the *hula noho* (seated *hula*) was to sit on the knees in a wide straddle position with the body firmly placed on the floor. We leaned and swayed with full energy. Our lifts were dictated by the earth and sky placements. If the hands rose, so did the whole body. The *waena* interludes were treated with serious concentration. Dancers of today would do well to continue this practice, as a beautifully executed *waena* is the strong cord that holds the dance together.

Kiʻi Pā Charts for Hula Hoʻokani
Charts for Rhythmic Interludes for Percussion *Hula*

At no time in the Beamer tradition are the elbows extended in a locked and tight position. When we took the beginning or final position of a *hula* Sweetheart Grandma would say, "Relax, exhale, form your bow position with 'soft' elbows."

ʻIliʻili (Pebbles)

Hoʻomākaukau (the preparation or ready pose)
Hold *ʻiliʻili* in hands as described below, both hands center forward, chest level, wrists crossed, palms up

Count	Action
1	Right hand reaches out to right side with left hand at center chest, palms up, lifting upward, click both hands and lean body right
2	Alternate, with left hand to left side (same as 1)
3 & 4	Both hands return to center at waist level. Roll hands around each other three times, click each time while leaning back

For our family, the *ʻiliʻili* had to be the correct size for our hands, that is, as long as the width of the palm and as wide as the *poho lima* (center of the palm). The primary *ʻiliʻili* is held between the index and middle fingers, resting in the palm. The secondary *ʻiliʻili* is tucked between the thumb and index fingers. The opening and closing of the hands is accomplished with strength, turning the body and head and lifting wrists with each *kiʻi pā*.

Kālāʻau (Sticks)

Hoʻomākaukau
Hold *kālāʻau* in hands, center forward, chest level, crossed at the center of the sticks, palms down

1	Tap forward center waist level, lean body forward
2	Tap center close to body at waist level, lean body back
3	Repeat 1
&	Repeat 2
4	Repeat 1

The *kālāʻau* sound changes with the dancer's light or tight grasp, which can be used very effectively to produce interesting tonal variations. Generally speaking, a relaxed wrist and gentle hold will sound and look better than a tight grip that produces a dull tone.

Pā Ipu (Hand Gourd Drum)

Hoʻomākaukau
Hold *ipu* forward, center chest level, in left hand with fingers of right hand at the *piko* (navel) of the *ipu*

1	Hit *ipu* with heel of right hand (downbeat)
2	Hit *ipu* with fingers of right hand (upbeat)
3	Hit *ipu* with heel of right hand (downbeat)
& 4	Hit *ipu* with fingers of right hand twice (upbeat), double-time
	Switch *ipu* to right hand and repeat same pattern with left hand

We were taught to say "u" (oo) for the downbeat and "te" (teh) for the upbeat. The downbeat is more heavily accented. The dancers lean their bodies in the direction of the *pa'i* (tap) motion as the story dictates. The *ki'i pā* for the (seated) *hula noho pā ipu* uses a leaning motion forward and back. In 1940 I taught standing *hula pā ipu*. I had not seen *hula pā ipu* performed in standing position. When I asked Sweetheart Grandma if I could, she said, "Why not." There are more than thirty different *ipu* rhythm patterns. The *ki'i pā* for the standing *hula* uses the same rhythm as for the *hula noho* but the body direction changes with the story.

Pū'ili (Bamboo Rattle)

Ho'omākaukau
Both hands center forward, chest level, palms down, *pū'ili* held in right hand with its tip resting on back of left fingers. Holding *pū'ili* in right hand, body sways in right clockwise circular movement. With *pū'ili* in left hand, body sways in left counterclockwise circular movement

1. Right hand taps on open palm of left hand as you lean body left
2. In a flowing motion *pū'ili* travels in an arc from left to right. Tap tip on floor at the forward right diagonal
3. Tap *pū'ili* on back of left hand, lean body back right
4. Place *pū'ili* on right shoulder (left hand forward at left diagonal, palm down), lean body left back diagonal

Repeat pattern holding *pū'ili* in left hand, body sways counterclockwise

Whatever we were taught with the right hand, we were expected to do as well with our left hand. Often when repeating verses we changed hands. Seated, single *hula pū'ili* was often danced facing each other in partners. The double *hula pū'ili*, both sitting and standing forms, are modern derivations. Body movements follow the story action: Land is low, sky is high, and so forth. Our general rule for sitting *hula* is to raise the body as we raise our hands from shoulder level in the storytelling.

Ūlili (Spinning Gourd Rattle)

1. Holding *ūlili* in left hand, pull *ūlili* string with right hand to the right, turning body to right side
2. Let *ūlili* string return quickly to the gourd in left hand, turning body to left side
3. Repeat 1
4. Repeat 2

'Ulī'ulī (Gourd Rattle)

Ho'omākaukau
Left hand on hip

1. With right fingers tap gourd on floor by right knee, say *"kahi"*
2. Repeat 1, say *"lua"*
3. Pick up gourd, say *"kolu"*
4. Place gourd on right lap (feathers up), say *"hā"*

Ki'i pā
Use same circular body roll as in *pū'ili ki'i pā*

1. Both arms are shoulder level, extended out forward diagonally, left palm down. Shake *'ulī'ulī* outward and in with right hand as left hand does hula wave
2. Brush *'ulī'ulī* outward on right knee
3. Brush *'ulī'ulī* on open palm of left hand from right to left
4. Brush open palm from left to right
5. Return gourd to right knee

We learned different styles of *ki'i pā* for *'ulī'ulī*. This is our favorite, Hilo style (or "Grandma's style"):

1. Both arms are shoulder level, extended out forward diagonally, left palm down. With *'ulī'ulī* in right hand, shake with full wrist, throw outward

&	Lift up (so seeds in gourd roll completely over)
2	Brush (not tap) right lap outward
&	Lift *ʻulīʻulī* up (gourd is at left side of right hand), feathers on the right side
3	Brush in left palm left to right (gourd is at right side of right hand)
&	Lift gourd up (gourd is at left side of right hand)
4	Repeat 3

In *hula ʻulīʻulī*, between verses when story gestures are not needed, the other hand would be extended forward in a simple *hula* wave and the body would rotate in a circular movement, being at the side where the gourd brushed the lap on the downbeat. Our Beamer method of holding the *ʻulīʻulī* is with thumb and middle finger touching so that the *ʻulīʻulī* moves freely up and down in the hand with relaxed fingers. Sweetheart Grandma did not allow us to "grip" the instrument with a tense wrist. The *ʻulīʻulī* hand was always relaxed and fluid. I do believe this technique gives us a richer sound, with the *aliʻipoe* seeds rolling more fully in the gourd.

Right-handed dancers hold the gourd in the right hand and vice versa. Generally speaking, left-handed students learned exactly as right-handed students. Grandma would often call out "*ʻākau*" (right) and "*hema*" (left) for us to change hands. She would expect us to alternate hands on each repeat of a verse. Sometimes it was boring doing each verse twice. And sometimes students had difficulty alternating hands. If this was the case they were allowed to perform using only their preferred hand.

Grandma did not teach us with double *ʻulīʻulī*; that was for a more modern time when my mother, Louise Leiomalama "Dambie" Beamer, began teaching in 1927. I have favored the older style *ʻulīʻulī* over the years. This instrument consists of the fruit of the *laʻamia* (calabash tree, *Crescentia cujete*), filled with *aliʻipoe* seeds and tied with an upright handle fashioned of thick, bound *lau hala* strips.

Grandma always told us that there was a great existing variety of styles for the *hula* folk to understand. We were made aware of the vast differences in interpretations of *hula*, and more and more over the years, I have come to honor and respect Sweetheart Grandma's loving embrace of all forms of the Hawaiian performing arts. Keep in mind always, "All knowledge does not live in your *hālau* (school) alone."

Protocol and *Hula* Formalities

Formality of ceremony and protocol is very important to the *hula* family. "Protocol" means the forms of ceremony and etiquette that are observed. *Hula* protocol is rigid and must be performed as tradition dictates. One of the most beautiful ceremonies I loved performing was the altar ritual.

Altar Ritual

We carried our *kī* (ti-leaf) skirts across our outstretched arms. On each skirt was placed the dancer's *lei poʻo* (head garland), *kūpeʻe lima* (hand wristlets), and *kūpeʻe wāwae* (anklets). If we were right-handed, the *lei ʻāʻī* (neck garlands) were draped over our right hands; if left-handed, over the left. With proper calls and responses, we entered with heads high and hearts pounding. We walked onto a dimly-lit stage dressed simply in a cotton chemise. What we wore was like a large pillowcase with the neck and arms cut out, its length reaching down to our knees. If a small group, we would sit on one side; if a large group, we would be divided, sitting diagonally on either side. We would kneel, placing our greenery directly in front of us, bending as far forward as we could in comfort.

Directly center upstage was a low *kuahu* (altar). This was decorated with *ʻieʻie* vines and rootlets, *hala*, *halapepe*, *ʻōhiʻa lehua* and various ferns—*ʻamaʻu*, *palapalai*, *uluhe*—on a base of ti leaves. In the center of this altar was positioned an uncarved block of *lama* wood. This was always provided by my dear father. Where he found the *lama* wood we never questioned. This grey piece of wood was mottled, somewhat porous and dried. Around this block of *lama* wood, to symbolize the presence of the *hula* goddess Laka, was swathed scented yellow tapa, draped and floating to the floor. To this day, the memory of this *kuahu* scene is vivid and tender. The altar became a living presence that breathed and exuded a pulsating *mana* (spiritual power). To a child this was both exciting and terrifying.

At a given signal, the *alakaʻi* (lead dancer) entered with a *pā halihali* (woven tray) on which had been placed small ti-leaf bundles of *pa'akai pu'upu'u* (coarse sea salt) to be offered at the altar. This somber ritual was performed with slow, fluid movements. Each *haumāna* (student) was offered a small bundle to give as a *ho'okupu* (gift). Some would take it and some not. If a dancer did not feel worthy at this time, the *kumu* (teacher) would not insist. I remember an instance when a member of our class, because she was menstruating and was uncomfortable, declined to take part in the ritual. We found out this reason after the performance was over. Grandma did not change expression or voice timbre, and everything else proceeded as scheduled as my friend sat in her place throughout the entire performance crying softly to herself. For those taking part in the ritual, we would approach the altar on our knees, deposit the ti-leaf bundles and crawl back to our places. I can remember getting sore knees.

An early recollection comes to mind of performing this ritual in the recreation hall of Haili Church, Hilo. I remarked to Sweetheart Grandma that it was beautiful enough to be performed at the pulpit. But in her wisdom she explained to us children that when we grew up, we would be in the sanctuary for other things, like our weddings and funerals.

Often when we were dancing, I was sure great-granduncle "Tūtū Bad Boy,"[2] the Reverend Stephen Desha of Haili Church, would bring his Christian wrath down upon us. He never did. I know it was his love for Sweetheart Grandma that gave him such tender compassion and tolerance for the *hula*.

Dressing Ritual

It is important here to note that all *hula* adornments must be made and cared for with the greatest of respect, from the time of picking the greenery to the time of performance. A *lei* should reflect a dancer's best work. *Hula* protocol dictates that if an adornment falls off during the performance, it should be left until the end and then discreetly removed. Respect for our adornments continues long after the performance is concluded; they should be lovingly and carefully returned to a nature setting from whence they came.

As a dressing chant began—sometimes it was Great Grandma's voice and sometimes Sweetheart Grandma's—I always had the feeling in my heart that I was in the forest and a gentle mist hovering over us was being dissipated by sunshine. It was a lovely thought, image and feeling. I could smell the cool, sweet air and even feel the earth under my feet.

At a given point in the chant, we began to lean forward to pick up our greenery. To begin the dressing ceremony, the ferns for our wrists would be put on first. Each dancer would lay the right wristlet over her right knee, place her right hand on it, palm up, and with the left hand, twist the ends of the wristlet and tuck it securely under the band. When that was complete, we held the wrist up with graceful fingers and a left tilt of the head to admire our handiwork. Then both hands were placed in a relaxed pose on the lap, palms up. The same procedure was followed for the left hand. Next came the anklets, beginning with the extension of the right foot diagonally forward, holding the anklet up as though admiring its beauty, bending to the right side, fastening the anklet at the back of the right ankle, returning the right foot to place and sitting back. At this point, there was a deep breath as we cupped our hands in our laps in a humble attitude. The same procedure then began for the left ankle.

After this, we began the placing of the head *lei*. We held up the head *lei,* leaning forward and then leaning back, arms above our heads. With chins lifted high, we placed the *lei po'o* on our brows firmly, then lowered the head and arms, placing the hands on our knees. Finally we raised our heads, lifted our shoulders and inhaled deeply. As we exhaled, the shoulders settled comfortably and we resumed the cupped palm position of hands in our laps.

At this point in the ritual, I found myself in a dreamlike trance. It was as though I was floating in a far-away place high above the clouds. Then Grandma's voice brought me back to reality. We were ready now for the *pā'ū lā'ī* (ti-leaf skirt). Sometimes for special occasions we wore *pā'ū heihei, hula* skirts decorated with leaves and ferns. We leaned forward, gently took both ends of the skirts, held them out and rose to our knees. We held the skirts to the right, leaned our bodies to the left and surveyed our beautiful handiwork. Then we brought the skirts forward in approval and repeated the

---

2. So called because, as a child, each time Tūtū saw my Papa he'd say "Cha, bad boy, bad boy." The name stayed with him all of his life.

same gesture to the left side as we leaned our bodies to the right. Following the nod of approval, we were ready to stand, first bringing the left foot up, then placing the right foot in a pointed pose, on the ball of the foot with all the toes touching the ground and the leg relaxed. I remember sometimes worrying about my knee trembling and whether the audience could see it. After tying the skirts securely at our backs, we were ready for the hand placement at the hips, fingers forward, thumbs back. As each of us returned the right foot, she placed the left foot in forward position and with her left hand lifted the left side of the skirt, repeating the same for the opposite side.

Now, bending to the far right, with right foot extended, we flexed the left knee and reached for the neck *lei*. Holding the *lei ʻāʻī* outstretched, we moved from the right to the left and back to center position. Next, stepping forward on the right foot we lifted the neck *lei* high, following the movement with our head and eyes. As we tilted the *lei* back to begin placing it on the shoulders, we changed the weight of our bodies to the left foot as our hands trailed down both sides of the *lei*. We followed with an inclining of the head as Grandma said the stirring words that end the Hiʻiaka *lei* chant, *"Ua ʻikea"* (see "Oli Lei," p. 31).

This was the crowning moment of the dressing ritual. *"ʻIke"* means to see, to know, to understand and to feel. *"Ua ʻikea"* means that it is known. This was an all-encompassing acknowledgment that we were fully aware of our deep commitment to the dance and fully prepared to accept the consequences. Were we going to be fine performers, stirring and heartfelt, or was our performance going to be mediocre and nondescript? How often I felt the tears rising, my heart close to overflowing at this dramatic moment. I always wanted to turn to Grandma and ask, "Is it okay? Will I be all right?"

Teaching and Choice of Materials

Since my early girlhood I have come to learn and more fully appreciate Sweetheart Grandma's careful choice of material. I am so proud to say that my teachers were members of my family and that my learning of *hula* came through my family, from Great Grandma to Sweetheart Grandma to Mother and me. It has always given me such a sense of joy and love. We were allowed to be children, acted like children and, of course, behaved like children. Sweetheart Grandma was firm but always kind and loving to us. Teaching children demands an extra portion of love, for the *kumu* (teacher) to enrich their lives with all the good their hearts can hold. Appropriate teaching material is vital at an early age. With adolescence will come more understanding and with maturity there is more appreciation. I commend conscientious *kumu* who select appropriate *hula keiki* (children's dances) for their students to learn.

Now, when I think back, I marvel that Sweetheart Grandma was so *akamai* (smart) about many teaching techniques. We learned to chant at the water's edge, following the wave action. She was constantly devising "teaching aids" to help us remember. For instance, this simple bit of advice, a sweet Helen Desha Beamer alliteration—"the tip of the tongue at the top of the teeth"—was a great learning tool for beginning chanters. When Sweetheart Grandma gave this bit of advice to an eight-year-old Beamer cousin, Mahi, he looked at her seriously and said, "But Grandma, I don't want to be a tounge tied tauboy" (tongue-tied cowboy). Sweetheart Grandma elaborated by explaining the importance of the actual shape of the mouth when speaking or chanting the Hawaiian language. The half-opened mouth produces a more native-sounding speech.

Mele Inoa

A *mele inoa* is a name chant, composed in honor of a person well known by the community. The most popular are the *mele inoa* composed for members of the royal families. In our family a *mele inoa* was often composed as a gift for a loved family member or a friend, and taken as a *hoʻokupu* (gift) to a baby *lūʻau* (feast) or to the host or hostess of a party. Baptisms, weddings and anniversaries were opportune occasions to offer a *mele inoa*. Our Beamer family files include more *mele inoa* than any other type of chant or song. This has always indicated to me that we had many beloved friends and family members. Cousin Marmionette Kaʻaihue published a book, *Songs of Helen Desha Beamer;* they are mostly *mele inoa*.[3]

In days of old, composition of a *mele* was often accomplished by a group rather than an individual.

---

3. Honolulu: Abigail K. Kawananakoa Foundation, 1991.

Once composed, the *mele inoa* became the property of the honoree. No one else could lay claim to it. At the death of an *ali'i* (chiefly) honoree, the next in line would often inherit the *mele inoa*. Thus, the vast majority of our legacy of Hawaiian literature does not bear the signature of its composers.

Some *mele inoa* were written to record a secret event, such as a love affair, without revealing the names of those involved. *Kake* were chants with coded words, mixed up or intentionally changed, some with inserted syllables and secret words. I remember dancing a *hula kake* with "ho" and "ha." It sounded so comical I struggled to keep my smile from turning into loud laughter. Sometimes the "ng" sound was used. I'm sure many other sounds were used in Hawaiian families, but over the years it has not been of interest to me to collect or decode these chants. If they were meant to be secretive, so be it.

Sweetheart Grandma had a personal name for me. I remember her chanting it at various times when we were alone, wrapping me in a towel after a bath or helping me change clothes. It was always soft and sweet, as though she were whispering to me. It was loving and very tender. I wish I had learned it.

Chants That Became Songs

Early in my teens, I began a battle of independence with my conscience. I loved the chants in any form and the *mele hula* were all very dear to me. Oftentimes, subconsciously in a moment of happiness, I found my heart singing a melody to a chant. I thought at first such improvisation was sacrilegious, but Sweetheart Grandma said it was a loving gift not be ignored. From these early years came melodies for the chants "Iā 'Oe E Ka Lā,"[4] "He Wahine Holo Lio" (p. 50), "Nohili" (pp. 70-71), "Ke Pohā Nei" (pp. 40-41), and so forth.

During my first formal teaching experience, in 1935 at Honolulu's Kaka'ako Mission School, I told the children the story of the *kāhuli* (land shells). As I did the chant, their eyes widened in fear. Suddenly I realized how spooky the chant sounded to the children and I quickly added one note. Their fear turned to smiles as the chant changed from minor mode to major key. I was convinced at that moment that a sweet melody was the key to helping children to enjoy a story. I have enjoyed that realization to this day.

It has not been uncommon over the years to learn of other composers setting traditional chants to melody. From the revered "Hole Waimea"[5] for Kamehameha I through the island songs of the Reverend Henry Waiau and the late contemporary composer Johnny Spencer, these songs are perhaps performed more widely because of their melodic content. I doubt if as many people would chant "Waikā" as would sing it. Of paramount importance is the message of the chant. Some listeners may not be able to relate to chant but their hearts may open to the message of the poetry set to music. I recently completed a *mele ma'i* (personal chant) for a production of son Keola. It began as a one-part chant and ended with three parts. It wasn't composed as a *mele inoa* (name chant) for anyone in particular, though as I was composing three specific dancers came to mind. As I was rereading it later, three lovely melodies surfaced—each melody was like the dancer I had in mind.

I wrote a chant, "Lei Kauna'oa,"[6] honoring the island of Lāna'i. As a Mother's Day present, Keola composed a lovely melody for this chant. When he recorded it, it became a very tender *mele hula*, giving more honor to the charming island of Lāna'i.

Translation, Transcription and Terminology

These translations have been written mostly by Mauli Cook, Kaliko Trapp and myself. We translated according to our own hearts and understanding, bringing the chants into clearer focus for us as well as the students. Our friend Pōhaku Nishimitsu was of invaluable assistance in further clarifying the elusive portions of many of these *mele hula*.

We are grateful to be able to turn to Hawai'i's beloved scholars Mary Kawena Pūku'i and Ka'upena Wong for their fine work.

Pūku'i and Elbert's *Hawaiian Dictionary* and *Place Names of Hawai'i* have been my principal references, thanks to the kind permission of the University of Hawai'i Press, along with Fornander,

---

4. See Nona Beamer, *Nā Mele Hula,* vol. 1, *A Collection of Hawaiian Hula Chants* (Lā'ie, Hawai'i: Institute for Polynesian Studies, 1987), pp. 34-35.

5. See Beamer, *Nā Mele Hula,* vol. 1, pp. 8-9

6. I have since learned that some of the *kūpuna* of Lāna'i refer to their island "flower" as *kauno'a.*

Honolulu January 2nd 1883

f.o.3	Mdse	Hart and Co			
	50 Bbls Molasses	@	4.-	200	
	50 Kegs Sugar 5000 ℔	"	9¢	450	650
f.o.3	Cash	W. Dill			
	Recv'd from him on deposit			500	
f.o.3	Dyer and Co	Mdse			
	5 Cords Wood	@	12.-	60	
f.o.3	Cash	Mdse			
	10 Cases K. Oil	@	3.-	30	
	1 Cord Wood			14	44
f.o.3	Mdse	Cash			
	12 Pairs Blankets	@	4.-	48	
	12 " Pants	"	3.-	36	
	12 Monkey Jackets	"	4.-	48	132
f.o.4	Hart and Co	Bills Payable			
	Amt our note Jan 2/83				
	at 3 mos in their favor			650	
f.o.3	Ship "Goodwill"	Mdse			
	10 Bbls flour	@	7.-	70	
	4 " Pork	"	25.-	100	
	4 " Beef	"	22.-	88	
	10 Tons Coal	"	15.-	150	
	1 Dz Axes			14	
	6 Bags Rice 600 ℔	"	6¢	36	
	10 Cases Bread 800 ℔	"	6¢	48	
	1 Bbl Hams			25	531
f.o.4	Ship "Goodwill"	Hon Bank'g Co			
	Gave Capt Bright check on				
	Bank as per his receipt			500	

This is a page from grandfather P. C. Beamer's store ledger.

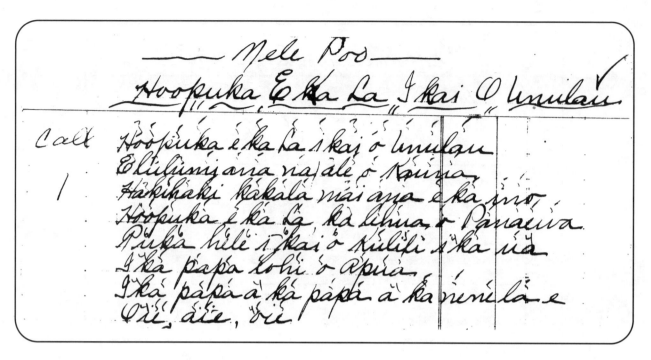

This is a page from Grandma's journal that was written on the back pages of Grandpa's hardware-store ledger. "Mele Poo" at the page's head is probably used here by Sweetheart Grandma to mean that this is a chant to be performed as the first in a formal program or exposition. I penciled in the numeric markings to indicate the chant melody. (See transcription of this chant on p. 36.)

Emerson, Kamakau and, of course, my dear Mother (see Bibliography).

Boxes and boxes of notes filled my office at Kamehameha Schools. Out of the myriad of folders a ledger of Sweetheart Grandma's came to light. What a treasure! We used Grandma's ledger as our source for chant texts, discovering additional verses she had penciled in, marginal notes and her number system for the chant melodies (see above). It was thrilling holding her notes from as far back as 1897 in my hand. The fronts of the ledger pages, written in beautiful, flowing Spencerian style (see p. 9), gave us a chuckle with purchases listed for nails, barrels of pork and so forth for Grandpa's Hilo store. What a precious legacy this ledger is of Sweetheart Grandma's *hula* knowledge. It is also such an exciting and tangible link with the past. How many documents like this lie forgotten in the dark closet corners of Hawaiian families throughout the world?

For many years now Kaliko, Mauli and I have labored with a new term for contemporary *hula kahiko*. We finally asked the assistance of Kalena Silva, chair of the Hawaiian Language Department at the University of Hawai'i at Hilo. He suggested *"hula 'aiakahiko"*—hula in the style of *kahiko*. Isn't that a great new Hawaiian word to add to our Hawaiian language! The word *"kahiko"* means the old style. The coupling of the word with *"'aia"* puts it in the present. Thus, *"'aiakahiko"* indicates a chant like the old style, written in these present times. Performing this kind of chant gives the *haku mele* (composer), teacher and student much more leeway for choreography, removing it from the strict formality of the *kahiko*. I know the term *"'aiakahiko"* will be enthusiastically embraced by the *hula* folk and all others. We have waited a long time for this new word. *Mahalo* Kalena!

Your own heart, as teacher and student, is of primary import. Your honest feelings and emotions expressed will make these chants come to life with joy and vitality. The words and sentiments are traditional. Your expression is part of our living inspiration. Only you can bring the chants to life, and you will be a shining example for all who see and hear you. Pass them on, in your own way, with your energy and precious love.

Part I

Nā Hana Hoʻohanohano

Rituals and Ceremonies

Nā Mele Oli No Laka
Chants for Laka

A ritual is a prescribed form for conducting a thoughtful ceremony. Ritual and ceremony are very important to the hula *family. The* kumu *(teacher) is not only disseminating traditional information, but also threading the essence of spirituality through the daily training. The* haumāna *(novitiates) learn that the spirit is a vital principle—the animating force that brings life and soul to the event. How can a people survive the rigors of existence without strong faith and the rituals that express that faith?*

These chants for the deity Laka serve to reinforce our belief in the importance of ritual as an integral part of the spirit of hula. *Laka was one of the patron gods/goddesses of the* hula. *The following chants reflect the emotional depth of the Hawaiian soul stirred in participant and observer alike. Is that not the purpose of belief?*

The sweet and humble devotion to the decoration of the altar gave us confidence that Laka was accepting the simple offering of our talent. Certainly, then, we were also worthy of sharing love!

Malu Ke Ala
The Path Is Cleared

The *kumu hula* (*hula* teacher) recites this prayer to clear the path of obstacles as the chanter and students proceed into the forest to gather greens for decorating the *hula* altar. It was a favorite prayer chant of Great Grandma's. She chanted it only for the older girls; perhaps the *keiki* (children) were too young to understand. Years later, we used it at the Queen's Surf Lū'au[1] in our opening ritual. Our *kahuna pule* (prayer expert), Ka'upena Wong, entered the performing area with this chant. He is one of the foremost and best-loved chanters of Hawai'i today. We always felt awed and humble when he made his entrance. *"'O au, 'o au nō"* was the concluding line we used as children; *"'O mākou, 'o mākou nō"* is used more commonly today.

Chant type: Pule (prayer)
Chant style: Kānaenae (prayerful)
Hula type: Ka'i Hele (processional walking entrance)

Noho ana ke akua i ka nāhelehele	The god dwells in the forest
I ālai 'ia e ke kī'ohu'ohu	Hidden away by the mists
E ka ua koko	And the low-lying blood-red rainbows
E nā kino malu i ka lani	O you spirits peaceful in the heavens
Malu e hoe	Shelter us as we walk
E ho'oulu mai ana 'o Laka[2] i kona kahu	Laka inspires her devotee
'O au, 'o au nō ā	Me, me indeed
['O mākou, 'o mākou nō ā]	[Us, us indeed]

1. Queen's Surf, the Waikīkī home of Mr. and Mrs. Chris Holmes (Aunt Mona Hind), was leased by the Spencecliff Corporation and converted into a garden restaurant, very popular with islanders and visitors alike in the 1950s and 60s. The Queen's Surf Lū'au, with Hawaiian ceremonies, originated here with the Beamer family hosting.
2. Patron deity of the *hula*, forest goddess whose plant forms include *maile (Alyxia olivaeformis)* and *laua'e* fern *(Phymatosorus scolopendria)*. Often regarded as a dual personality with the goddess Kapo. "Kapo and Laka were one in spirit, though their names were two" (quoted in Nathaniel B. Emerson, *Unwritten Literature of Hawaii: The Sacred Songs of the Hula* [reprint, Rutland, Vt.: Charles E. Tuttle, 1965], p. 47). Occasionally referred to as a male god.

Pule No Ke Akua 'O Laka
Prayer to the Goddess Laka

Because Laka is one of the patron deities of the *hula*, many prayers are dedicated to her. The *maile*[1] and *'ie'ie* vines[2] are among Laka's *kino lau* (physical forms). Accompanied by the appropriate *oli*, the *hula* altar is adorned with these *kino lau* and an uncarved block of *lama* wood,[3] another symbol of the goddess's presence. All was in readiness for the next phase of ritual prayers to begin. The beauty of the *lama* wood draped in a long graceful wrap of yellow *kapa* (bark cloth) inspired a reverence in my heart that I have carried with me all my life. Often Grandma would adjust the tapa as she chanted. One of my earliest questions was, "Who is Laka?" Grandma explained that Laka is an *'aumakua* (family god) of the *hula* family, further saying she was "one of God's handmaidens." That imagery was perfect in my childlike religious scheme of things holy and satisfied my inquisitive mind: Laka is the goddess of the wildwood and thus a special goddess of the *hula*. After the Laka prayer, we would remove our *lei po'o* and *lei 'ā'ī* (head and neck garlands) and place them on the altar.

Chant type:　　Pule (prayer)
Chant style:　　Kānaenae (prayerful)
Hula type:　　[None]

'O Laka ke ali'i o nu'u	Laka is highest of all chiefs
Ō mai	Answer my call
'O Laka mai uka	Laka of the mountain
'O Laka mai kai	Laka of the sea
Ho'onani ka wahine nui	We honor the greatest among women
Nāna e ha'iha'i i ka 'ohu o ka 'ie'ie	Who breaks the mist of the *'ie'ie*
Ka maile hihi o ka nahele	And the entangled *maile* of the forest
E hui ho'i a hau'oli	Join once again with happiness
'O 'oe 'o Ha'ikamālamalama[4]	You are Ha'ikamālamalama
'O Hina[5] wahine ke akua hula nui ē	Hina great *hula* goddess
E ho'i mai ē	Return

1. A native twining shrub *(Alyxia olivaeformis)*.
2. An endemic Hawaiian woody, branching climber *(Freycinetia arborea)* that grows at higher altitudes.
3. Hawaiian ebony *(Diospyros* or *Maba)*, used in medicine and placed on *hula* altars as its name suggests enlightenment.
4. Lit., tells of the enlightenment; probably an ancient Hawaiian female deity.
5. The name "Hina" is given to many important female deities in Hawai'i, associated with various aspects of the culture; the most well known Hina is the goddess who resides in the moon.

Eia Au E Laka
Here I Am O Laka

This was one of a large body of Laka poems we used as entrance chants. Great Grandma chanted it in a very solemn manner. We carried *lei* of *palapalai*[1] with which to honor Laka and Hiʻiaka. It made us feel humble and reverent to kneel before the altar. Walking or seated, this chant has a special prayerful place in our *hula* repertoire.

Chant type: Pule (prayer)
Chant style: Kānaenae (prayerful)
Hula type: Noho (seated), Kaʻi Hele (processional walking entrance)

Eia au e Laka	Here I am O Laka
E Kāne[2] a Haʻiwahine[3]	O Kāne belonging to Haʻiwahine
Hoʻouluulu lei o Laka	At the *hula* altar of Laka
ʻO Hiʻiaka[4] ke kāula	Hiʻiaka is the prophetess
Nāna i ʻaʻe a ulu	It is she who goes atop and inspires
Noho i kō kahua	And dwells in your foundation site
Eia ka wai lā he wai ola	Here is the water a water of life
E ola iaʻu iā kākou nō a pau	Life to me to us all indeed

1. A native fern *(Microlepia setosa)*.
2. God of creation, sunlight, fresh water and forests.
3. Probably an ancient female deity.
4. One of a number of younger sisters of Pele, all named Hiʻiaka; most probably this refers to the youngest sister, Hiʻiakaikapoliopele, who was worshiped as a *hula* goddess.

Kānaenae No Laka
A Prayer Chant for Laka

As youngsters we used this chant frequently, although Sweetheart Grandma never expected us to memorize all of it. The complete chant and translation is found in Nathaniel B. Emerson's *Unwritten Literature of Hawaii*,[1] as shown here with added diacritical markings. Because of the great love for this chant that Sweetheart Grandma instilled in my heart, I used it as a young adult at the Queen's Surf Lū'au. If the skies darkened and threatened rain, I would chant this *mele oli* (poem to be chanted) in hope that Laka would bless us and make things right.

Chant type: Inoa (name)
Chant style: Kānaenae (prayerful)
Hula type: Ka'i Huaka'i (formal processional with gestures)

A ke kuahiwi i ke kualono	In the forest on the ridges
Kū ana 'o Laka i ka mauna	Of the mountains stands Laka
Noho ana 'o Laka i ka po'o o ka 'ohu	Dwelling in the source of the mist
'O Laka kumu hula	Laka teacher of the *hula*
Nāna i 'a'e ka waokele	Has climbed the rain forest of the gods
Kahi kahi i mōlia i ka pua'a	Altars hallowed by the sacrificial swine
I ke po'o pua'a	The head of the boar
He pua'a hiwa na Kāne[2]	The black boar of Kāne
He kāne na Laka	A partner he with Laka
Na ka wahine i 'oni a kelakela i ka lani	Woman she by strife gained rank in heaven
I kupu ke a'a i ke kumu	That the root may grow from the stem
I lau a puka ka mu'o	That the young shoot may put forth and leaf
Ka liko ka 'ao i luna	Pushing up the fresh unfolded bud

1. Reprint, Rutland, Vt.: Charles E. Tuttle, 1965, pp. 16-18.
2. One of the four principal Hawaiian gods; god of life and light.

Kupu ka lālā hua ma ka hikina	The scion-thrust bud and fruit toward the east
Kupu ka lā'au 'ona a Makali'i[3]	Like the tree that bewitches the winter fish
'O Mākālei[4] lā'au kaulana mai ka pō[5] mai	Mākālei tree famed from the age of night
Mai ka pō mai ka 'oia'i'o	Truth is the counsel of night
I hō'i'o i luna i o'o i luna	May it fruit and ripen above
He luna au e ki'i mai nei iā 'oe	A messenger I bring you
E Laka	O Laka
E ho'i ke kākua pā'ū	To the girding of skirt
He lā 'ūniki no kāua	An opening fiesta this for thee and me
Hā'ike'ike o ke Akua	To show the might of the God
Hō'ike ka mana o ka Wahine	The power of the Goddess
'O Laka kaikuahine	Of Laka the sister
Wahine a Lonoika'ouali'i[6]	To Lono a wife in the heavenly courts
E Lono	O Lono
E hui 'ia mai ka lani me ka honua	Join heaven and earth
Nou 'oko'a Kūkuluokahiki[7]	Thine alone are the Pillars of Kahiki
Me ke 'ano'ai aloha ē	Warm greetings beloved one
E aloha ē	Greetings

3. Lit., little eyes; the constellation Pleiades; also the winter season, marked by the rising of the constellation in the east at sunset.
4. Supernatural tree of Moloka'i; its roots were said to attract fish.
5. The time of darkness before the world as we know it was created.
6. One of the four principal Hawaiian gods; god of the harvest.
7. A vertical wall along the horizon at Tahiti that supports the sky in traditional Hawaiian cosmology.

Pule Kuahu
Altar Prayer

The *pule kuahu* are a formal, sacred group of ceremonial chants especially for praying at the *hula* altar. This one was used while decorating the altar of the *hula* goddess Laka. We brought in *lehua*,[1] *'ie'ie* vines,[2] *halapepe*,[3] *kī*[4] and countless armsful of *laua'e*,[5] *pala'ā*[6] and *palapalai*[7] fern. Everything smelled so fresh and sweet. Fragrances are very special to Hawaiians, being an important spiritual link with our past that brings all the yesterdays to the fore. Although this is a *pule kuahu*, Sweetheart Grandma chanted it at times in a fashion appropriate for *hula*. We danced it as a *hula 'ōhelo* (reclining), *hula noho* (seated) or *hula 'ōlapa* (standing). This was very exciting to perform.

Chant type: Pule (prayer)
Chant style: Kānaenae (prayerful)
Hula type: [Usually none, but could be 'Ōhelo (reclining), Noho (seated) or 'Ōlapa (standing)]

Noho ana 'o Laka i ka uluwehiwehi	Laka dwells amidst the forest green
Kū ana i luna o Mo'ohela'ia[8]	Standing there above Mo'ohela'ia
'Ōhi'a kū[9] i luna o Maunaloa[10]	The *'ōhi'a kū* fern above Maunaloa
Aloha mai Kaulana'ula[11] ia'u	Love from Kaulana'ula to me
Eia ka 'ula lā	Here is the sacred [spirit] thing
He 'ūlāleo	It is a [chant] calling appeal
He uku he mōhai	A tribute an offering
He kānaenae	A supplication prayer
A pono au	May all be right with me
A pono kāua	That it may also be right for us both

1. The flower of the *'ōhi'a* tree *(Metrosideros macropus, M. collina* subsp. *polymorpha)*; also the tree itself.
2. An endemic Hawaiian woody, branching climber *(Freycinetia arborea)*.
3. Native tree in the lily family *(Dracaena [Pleomele] aurea)*, used in *hula* and other religious ceremonies.
4. Ti, a woody plant in the lily family *(Cordyline terminalis)*, of many and varied uses to the Hawaiian people and believed to have spiritual power.
5. A particularly fragrant fern *(Phymatosorus scolopendria)*; crushed, its fragrance suggests that of *maile*.
6. A lacy fern *(Sphenomeris chinensis)*.
7. A native fern *(Microlepia setosa)*.
8. Place name of undetermined location, perhaps near Maunaloa, Moloka'i.
9. Lit., standing [on] *'ōhi'a;* a native fern that grows on trees in damp forests *(Mecodium recurvuum)*.
10. Land division in western Moloka'i.
11. Lit., the famous red[ness]; fig., the setting place of the sun: the name of a deity belonging to the order *(papa)* of the *hula* (Nathaniel B. Emerson, *Unwritten Literature of Hawaii: The Sacred Songs of the Hula* [reprint, Rutland, Vt.: Charles E. Tuttle, 1965], p. 33).

Pule Hoʻonoa
A Prayer to Lift Sacred Restrictions

I remember this prayer with joy. I do not recall another like it. The rhythmic clapping stimulated us mentally and physically. The clapping brought a sense of urgency and a surge of energy as we put our minds and hearts in the mood of prayer.

Chant type: Pule (prayer), Inoa (name)
Chant style: Kānaenae (prayerful)
Hula type: Paʻi Lima (hand clapping)

Pūpū weuweu e Laka ē	A chant prayer for you O Laka
ʻO kona weuweu ke kū nei	Her sacred greenery stands here
Kaumaha aʻela iā Laka ē	An offering to Laka
ʻO Laka ke akua pule ikaika	Laka is the goddess of the powerful prayer
Ua kū ka maile[1] a Laka a i mua	The *maile* of Laka stands out foremost
Ua lū ka hua	The seeds have been scattered
Hua o ka maile	The seeds of the *maile*
Noanoa iaʻu iā Kahaʻula[2]	Freed freed by me, by Kahaʻula
Pāpālua noa	A double freedom
Noa a ua noa	Freedom freedom is complete
ʻEliʻeli kapu ʻeliʻeli noa	A taboo profound a freedom profound
Kapu ʻoukou kapu ke akua	You are sacred the god is sacred
Noa mākou noa ke kanaka	We are free one and all
"HE INOA NO LAKA"	"In the name of Laka"

---

1. A native twining shrub *(Alyxia olivaeformis);* one of the principal plants used in *hula* worship and a *kino lau* (physical form) of Laka.
2. Goddess who presides over erotic dreams.

Nā Mele Oli No Ka Hoʻomākaukau ʻAna
Chants in Preparation for *Hula*

Our performances were special reasons to observe the formalities and protocol of the hula. *The* hoʻomākaukau, *preparation, was a most fascinating and exciting feature. One does not simply saunter casually onto the hula stage. The entrance is meticulous, formal and very serious. Calls are uttered and answered, asking permission to approach, then to enter. Thus, reverence and honor are instilled in the heart of the dancer.*

The graciousness of welcoming strangers into my heart and filling my family home with love, the humility of asking—pleading—to be allowed to perform, brought me in touch with my feelings of the moment. Finally, dressing myself carefully for the performance ahead—with the anklets, wristlets, skirt and lei *all made with great care and now adorning my body—made me feel like the most beautiful child in the whole world!*

Kūnihi Ka Mauna
The Mountain Stands Steep

The *oli kāhea* are a group of chants asking permission to enter the *hula* school. Standing on the stone steps at Halehuki, Grandma's Hilo home, our *hula* line stretched beyond the cluster of torch gingers and a bamboo thicket to the mango tree. The rushing sound of the Wailuku River cascaded tumultuously below and we had to chant loudly to be heard over the din. This calling chant, from the island of Kaua'i, is of an older vintage, probably from Great Grandma, Isabella Ka'ili Desha. Sweetheart Grandma usually chanted her own original *oli kāhea* that were sweet and personal; fragments remain in my memory.

Chant type: Kāhea (calling out), Wahi Pana (place), Ka'i (entrance)
Chant style: Ho'olaha (declarative)
Hula type: Ka'i (entrance)

Kūnihi ka mauna i ka la'i ē	The mountain stands steep in the calm
'O Wai'ale'ale[1] lā i Wailua[2]	Wai'ale'ale is at Wailua
Huki a'ela i ka lani	Pulled upward towards the heavens
Ka papa 'auwai o Kawaikini[3]	Is the stream bridge of Kawaikini
Ālai 'ia a'ela e Nounou[4]	Blocked by Nounou is the view
Nalo Kaipuha'a[5]	Kaipuha'a hill is lost
Ka laulā ma uka o Kapa'a[6] ē	[It is] the broad expanse upland of Kapa'a
Mai pa'a i ka leo	Do not hold back your voice
He 'ole ka hea mai ē	There is no answer in reply

1. Lit., rippling or overflowing water; highest mountain on Kaua'i.
2. Lit., two waters; river, valley and town near Līhu'e.
3. Lit., multitudinous waters; highest peak on Wai'ale'ale.
4. Lit., throwing; mountain now known as Sleeping Giant, trail and forest reserve in the Kawaihau district of Kaua'i.
5. Lit., the low calabash; hill in the Kawaihau district, Kaua'i.
6. Lit., the solid or the closing; land division in eastern Kaua'i.

Oli Aloha
Chant of Loving Welcome

To inspire the spirit of welcome in our chanting, Sweetheart Grandma told us this charming vignette: "Think of a very special place that really fills your heart. Imagine yourself in that place. Feel the air, smell its freshness, fill your eyes with the beauty and let it rest deep in your soul. Utter your sweetest tone. Let it reverberate so it fills your entire body and overflows to fill this special place. Now, invite a loved friend to come into your space. Feel the glow of love as that special person comes toward you. Your heart lifts, your eyes warm with recognition and your arms are eager to embrace your friend. As you walk together in the forest, the mist begins to lift and sunlight enters. Your hearts have warmed the place and love has come in. *Aloha ē, aloha ē* . . . May love be with you, may love be with you."

Chant type: Heahea (welcome)
Chant style: Hoaaloha (loving friendship)
Hula type: Kaʻi Huakaʻi (formal processional with gestures)

Onaona i ka hala me ka lehua[1]	Fragrant with pandanus and *lehua*
He hale lehua nō ia na ka noe	It is a house of *lehua* made by the mist
ʻO kaʻu nō ia e ʻanoʻi nei	There is that which I desire
E liʻa nei hoʻi ʻo ka hiki mai	Which I indeed have a yearning for and that is the arrival
A hiki mai nō ʻoukou	And indeed you all have come to me
A hiki pū nō me ke aloha	And you have come together with hearts full of love
Aloha ē	May love be with you
Aloha ē	May love be with you

1. The flower of the *ʻōhiʻa* tree (*Metrosideros macropus, M. collina* subsp. *polymorpha*); also the tree itself. It is frequently used as a metaphor in Hawaiian poetry and song, and here perhaps symbolizes a man in a romantic relationship with his sweetheart, represented by the *hala* (pandanus).

Aloha Nā Hale
Beloved Are the Houses

This is an *oli komo* (welcome chant) we used as children to welcome our fellow *hula* students as they came to our home for class. We did not chant to welcome adults, as we were only children without proper authority to turn our house over to others. At Sweetheart Grandma's home, Halehuki, she and Great Grandma often chanted to greet visitors. These chants were frequently tearful as well as poetic and heartfelt. They were expressions of joy upon the visit of a loving family member or friend. There were always warm, generous hugs and kisses. Years later, when I lived in Kona and had special days with our dear 'Iolani Luahine, one of Hawai'i's greatest *hula* exponents, I was to learn of other entrance chants more frequently used today.

Chant type: Komo (invitation to enter)
Chant style: Hoaaloha (loving friendship)
Hula type: [None]

Nona's:

Aloha nā hale o mākou	Beloved are our houses
I makamaka 'ole	Now empty of dear friends
Ke alanui hele	Proceeding along the path
Ma uka o Pu'ukāhea[1] lā ē	Inland of Pu'ukāhea
Kāhea	Call out
E kāhea aku ka pono ē	Call out the proper way
Komo mai 'oe i loko nei	Enter within and be welcome
Eia ka pu'u nui o waho nei	Here is the great discomfort of being outside
He anu	The cold

'Iolani's:

E hea i ke kanaka	Call to the person
E komo ma loko	Come in
E hānai ai a hewa ka waha	Eat until your mouth can take no more
Eia nō ka uku lā 'o ka leo	Here is the reward—the voice
A he leo wale nō	A voice only
'Ae	Yes

1.   Lit., calling hill; land sections in Hālawa, Moloka'i, and in Wai'anae, O'ahu.

Eia Hawai'i
Behold Hawai'i

This is a traditional chant of great historical importance. Imagine those seafaring canoes coming into Hilo Bay, the emotion of landfall after their long journey, and the chanter, Kamahu'alele,[1] standing on the platform of a double-hulled canoe making this historic pronoucement. The complete chant can be found in Fornander's *An Account of the Polynesian Race.*[2] The following lines were the ones taught to us by Sweetheart Grandma.

Chant type: Ka'i (entrance), Wahi Pana (place)
Chant style: 'Oli'oli (joyous)
Hula type: Ka'i Hele (processional walking entrance)

Eia Hawai'i he moku he kanaka	Behold Hawai'i an island a man
He kanaka Hawai'i ē	A Hawaiian man
He kanaka na Tahiti[3]	A man of Tahiti
Iā Papa[4] i hānau	Papa gave birth to him
'O Mō'īkeha[5] lani nāna e noho	Mō'īkeha is the chief who shall rule
Noho ku'u lani iā Hawai'i	My chief shall rule Hawai'i
Noho iā Hawai'i a lūlana	Rule Hawai'i and live in peace

1. Lit., child of the flying sea spray; ancient priest and navigator.
2. Reprint, Rutland, Vt.: Charles E. Tuttle, 1969, pp. 10-11.
3. Island chain in the South Pacific; origin of voyage.
4. Earth mother.
5. Famous high chief, bard and navigator.

Hālau Waiʻanae
Waiʻanae Longhouse

This was one of Great Grandma's favorite chants. It was the first I remember hearing her chant. She would always get a faraway look in her eyes, as if she were dreaming lovingly of an earlier day. She lived in Waiʻanae, on the leeward coast of Oʻahu, and wrote this *mele* (poem) to recount her experience on seeing a *haole* (foreigner) for the first time. As Great Grandma lay dying in 1949, in her great *koa*[1] wood bed, she raised her frail body and chanted this *mele*. Sweetheart Grandma loved this chant so much she used lines 6 to 8 in her composition "Kawohikūkapulani."

Chant type: Kaʻi (entrance), Wahi Pana (place)
Chant style: Olioli (formal), Mailani (sweet praise)
Hula type: Kaʻi Hele (processional walking entrance)

Hālau Waiʻanae molale i ka lā

Ala pono i ke kula ʻo Kūmanomano[2]
Kūnihi ka noho a Maunalahilahi[3]
Hoʻomaha aku i ka wai o Lualualei[4]
Lei ana Nuʻuanu[5] i ke kāmakahala[6]

I paukū ʻia me ka ʻāhihi[7]
I hoʻohihi nō au naʻu ʻoe
Koʻu kuleana paʻa nō ia
He ʻike haole
E lūlū lima ke aloha ē

At the longhouse of Waiʻanae shining in the sun

The true path to the plains of Kūmanomano
Mount Lahilahi a steep ascent
There we rested near the stream of Lualualei
Nuʻuanu is wreathed in garlands of *kāmakahala*

Entwined with the *ʻāhihi lehua*
I greatly admire you and you are mine
You are mine bound firmly to me forever
When you see the stranger
Extend the hand of love

1. The largest of native forest trees *(Acacia koa)*.
2. A bur grass *(Cenchrus agrimonioides)*; possibly the place name of the area.
3. Lit, thin or delicate mountain; place inland of the sea at Mākaha, on the Waiʻanae Coast.
4. Area just south of Waiʻanae town and valley.
5. Valley in Honolulu.
6. All species of a native genus *(Labordia)* of forest trees and shrubs.
7. Low-spreading bush *(Metrosideros sp.)* related to *lehua*, formerly numerous in Nuʻuanu.

Oli Kūpeʻe
Chant for Wristlets and Anklets

This is one of the traditional *oli kūpeʻe* performed today. Our *oli kūpeʻe* were in the same style as the skirt chants, personal and loving. I have many happy recollections of fastening my wristlets and anklets: the sounds of soft, gentle words, the sweet forest fragrance of ferns and the wonderful feeling of accomplishment in fashioning my *hula* adornments. After many hours of gathering, sorting and weaving, your golden hour arrives. You are showing your handiwork, holding your breath, praying that the *lei* you have so lovingly fashioned will not fall apart with your first movement.

Chant type: Hoʻokāhiko (adorning)
Chant style: Mailani (sweet praise)
Hula type: [None]

ʻAʻala kupukupu i ka uka o Kānehoa[1]	The mountains of Kānehoa are fragrant with ferns
E hoa	May they be bound firmly
Hoa nā lima o ka makani	Hands bind like the wind
He Waikōloa[2]	A Waikōloa wind
He Waikōloa ka makani	It is a Waikōloa wind
Anu Līhuʻe[3]	That chills Līhuʻe
ʻĀlina lehua i kau ka ʻōpua	Battered are the *lehua* as the cloud bank rises
Kuʻu pua	My cherished blossom
Kuʻu pua ʻiʻini e kui a lei	My flower a desired blossom to be strung in a garland
Inā iā ʻoe ka leia mai la	If only you were a cherished garland for me to wear

1. Lit, companion [of] Kāne; hill in Wahiawā, Oʻahu.
2. A cool wind that blows in Līhuʻe, Kauaʻi; also possibly in Wahiawā, Oʻahu.
3. Lit, cold chill; district in Kauaʻi; also a former land section in Wahiawā, Oʻahu. Many islands share some of the same place names.

Oli Pāʻū
Skirt Chant

This is one of the traditional *oli pāʻū* heard today. Great Grandma, however, chanted the *oli pāʻū* in a spontaneous style, not memorized word for word but geared to the occasion. It might be a *kīkepa* (tapa sarong) we were tying at our left shoulder, or a fresh *pāʻū lau kī* (ti-leaf skirt) to tie at our waist. We always wore a simple cotton shift as our undergarment when we wore ti-leaf skirts. I do not see dressing taking place on stage today. Perhaps it is too slow for contemporary performances. I do so long for the complete grace of the dressing chants, when, oblivious of all others present, we seemed the only ones there.

Chant type: Komo Lole (dressing)
Chant style: Mailani (sweet praise)
Hula type: [None]

Kākua pāʻū ʻahu nā kīkepa	Bind tightly the skirt—drape the tapa on your shoulder
I ka pāʻū noʻenoʻe i hoʻoluʻu ʻia	The skirt that has been printed and dyed
I hoʻokākua ʻia a paʻa	Let the skirt be bound tightly
I luna o ka imu	Above the earth oven
Kū ka huʻa o ka pali o Kawaikapu[1]	The froth and foam rises at the base of Kawaikapu cliff
He kuʻina pāʻū pali no Kupehau[2]	The five layers of the skirt resembling the ridges of Kupehau
I holo a paʻa ʻia	Continue until it is tight
A paʻa e Honokāne[3]	Tightened by Honokāne

This is a sample of one of our spontaneous dressing chants:

Kēia ʻala o ka pāʻū kī	Here now the sweet fragrance of the ti skirt
Ua maʻū me ka līhau	Moistened by the gentle rain
Mai nā ulu lāʻau	From the forests
Ua hana ʻia me kuʻu lima aloha	Made with my loving hands
ʻO au nō he mea i ʻāpono ʻia	May I be acceptable

1. Lit, the sacred water; place name, location unknown.
2. Mountain located in Waipiʻo Valley, Hawaiʻi island. The skirt folds are likened to the ridges and valleys of the mountains.
3. Lit., bay of Kāne; land division and stream at Waipiʻo.

Oli Lei
Lei Chant

Grandma used spontaneous, personal chants when making *lei* presentations. However, this traditional *oli lei* was the chant we used as the finale of the dancers' dressing ritual.[1] It is perhaps the most revered of the many *lei* chants, as it was part of the repertoire of the Pele family, in the oratory of Hi'iakaikapoliopele, the volcano goddess's favorite sister. Cousin Mahi Beamer chants this with such love and tenderness. I see Sweetheart Grandma in his eyes and hear her in his voice. What joy!

Chant type: Hoʻokāhiko (adorning)
Chant style: Olioli (formal), Hoʻonānā (soothing)
Hula type: Kuhi Lima (gesture)

Ke lei maila ʻo Kaʻula[2] i ke kai	Kaʻula is encircled by the ocean with a garland of sea foam
Ka mālamalama o Niʻihau ua mālie	Niʻihau shines brightly amidst gentle seas
A mālie pā ka Inuwai[3]	When the calm has come the Inuwai wind blows
Ke inu maila nā hala o Naue[4] i ke kai	The pandanus of Naue drink from the sea
No Naue ka hala, no Puna ka wahine[5]	From Naue the pandanus, from Puna the woman
No ka lua nō i Kīlauea[6]	From the pit indeed at Kīlauea
Ua ʻikea	Let it be known

1. See Introduction, pp. 6-7.
2. Rocky islet southwest of the island of Niʻihau.
3. A sea wind.
4. Place near Hāʻena in the Haleleʻa district of Kauaʻi.
5. Reference to Pele; Puna, famous for being the site of volcanic activity, is often mentioned in chants as a favorite forest area of hers.
6. Active volcano on Hawaiʻi island.

Part II

Nā Mele Hula

Dance Chants

Pele The Fire Goddess

I was angry with Pele when I first danced for her at Halemaʻumaʻu Crater, her home in the firepit of Kīlauea Volcano. Sweetheart Grandma had told us that Kīlauea meant "erupting, spewing lava," and I anticipated tumultuous noise and terrifying feelings. My heart began to pound as I stepped out of Grandma's old brown station wagon. We tied on our hula skirts. Aunt Harriett, Papa's older sister, tugged at each to make sure they were secure. It was cold and windy. I was scared.

Aunty Kawohi, Papa's youngest sister, stepped out confidently, without hesitation. She was older than I and accustomed to my habit of squeezing in behind her. But that day, she seemed annoyed with my cowering. Grandma put me bodily in a center-front position.

The energetic chorus of "ʻOaka Ē Ka Lani" rang out, but my skirt was not moving with the dance. If Pele wanted me to dance, I thought, the goddess of fire and the volcano should help me move my skirt. I left my position and walked to Grandma's side. "Pele doesn't want me to dance," I pouted. Oh yes, I was huhū (angry) with Pele.

Hoʻopuka Ē Ka Lā I Kai O Unulau
The Sun Rises over the Sea of Unulau

This well-loved traditional entrance chant speaks poetically of many of the Big Island places associated with Pele. Sweetheart Grandma choreographed descriptive gestures and entrance steps used only for this chant. In contrast, the foot patterns and nondescriptive gestures she had us use for "Hoʻopuka Ē Ka Lā Ma Ka Hikina" (The Sun Rises in the East)[1] were also used with other entrance chants, for example, "ʻO Ke Mele Mua Kēia O Ka Hula Pele."[2] As students, it was exciting to have two groups entering from either side of the stage, simultaneously dancing to both "Hoʻopuka" chants and chanting our hearts out happily.

Chant type:	Hoʻomaikaʻi (praise), Pule (prayer)
Chant style:	Kānaenae (prayerful), Mailani (sweet praise)
Hula type:	Kaʻi (entrance), Kuʻi (interpretive)

Kāhea	Kumu:	"Hoʻomākaukau"
	Haumāna:	" ʻAe, hoʻopuka ē ka lā i kai o Unulau"

Hoʻopuka ē ka lā i kai o Unulau[3]	The sun rises seaward of Unulau
E lulumi ana nā ʻale o Kaunā[4]	Churning are the waves of Kaunā
Hakihaki kākala mai ana ē ka ʻino	Roughly broken by the coming of the storm
Hoʻopuka ē ka lā i ka lehua[5] o Panaʻewa[6]	The sun rises [over] the *lehua* blossoms of Panaʻewa
Puka hele i kai o Kūlili[7] i ka ua	It continues to rise in the rain seaward of Kūlili
I ka papa lohi o ʻĀpua[8]	On the shining plains of ʻĀpua
I ka papa a ka Papaakanēnē[9] lā	To the flats of Papaakanēnē
ʻOie aie ʻoie aie ē ē ē ē	Tra la la la
"HE INOA NO HIʻIAKAIKAPOLIOPELE"	"A chant in honor of Hiʻiaka-in-the-bosom of Pele

1. See Nona Beamer, *Nā Mele Hula,* vol. 1, *A Collection of Hawaiian Hula Chants* (Lāʻie, Hawaiʻi: Institute for Polynesian Studies, 1987), pp. 70–71.
2. See next page.
3. Name of a place at Kaʻū, Hawaiʻi.
4. Point in southwestern Kaʻū, about halfway between Hoʻōpūloa and South Point.
5. Flower of the *ʻōhiʻa* tree. Legends relate that a man who refused Pele's amorous advances was turned into an *ʻōhiʻa* tree. The gods, taking pity on his sweetheart, turned her into a beautiful red *lehua* flower blooming on the tree.
6. Land division near Hilo.
7. Probably a place name on Hawaiʻi island.
8. Lit., fish basket; land division and point in Puna.
9. Lit., *nēnē* (geese) flats; a place, probably in Puna.

ʻO Ke Mele Mua Kēia O Ka Hula Pele
The First Chant of the Pele Dances

We always gathered before performances to ask our Father in heaven to bless us, that we might do our very best. At the conclusion of the prayer, Grandma would smile sweetly and whisper intently, telling us what to do next. Her words would be something like this: "Pele is waiting for us. Let us put our hearts and minds in a Pele mood and talk with her. She has much to tell us, we must listen and feel her power." Then we would make our entrance with this chant. This was one of our favorite entrance chants preceding the *hula Pele*. It is performed in a formal style with erect posture and dignity. In the dancer, pride is of great import. The chant tones are uttered in a sincere, meaningful manner as though reciting the classic genealogy of the revered Pele family.

Dancing at the firepit of Halemaʻumaʻu[1] at Kīlauea Crater was a childhood must. Knotting my ti-leaf skirt was a happy activity. I loved the smell of the leaves and would pull on the stems to make them stick out as far as I could all around my waist. When it was time to dance, the wind would rise magically and we would be hushed and awed.

Chant type: Kaʻi (entrance)
Chant style: Mailani (sweet praise)
Hula type: Pele (volcano goddess), Kaʻi Huakaʻi (formal processional with gestures)

Mai Kahiki[2] ka wahine ʻo Pele
Mai ka ʻāina ʻo Polapola[3]
Mai ka pūnohu ʻula a Kāne[4]
Mai ke ao lalapa i ka lani
Mai ka ʻōpua ʻōlapa i Kahiki

"HE INOA NO PELE"

From Kahiki came the woman Pele
From the land of Bora Bora
From the red mist of Kāne
From the cloud blazing in the heavens
From the fiery cloud pile of Kahiki

"A name chant for Pele"

1. Lit., house of the *ʻamaʻu* fern *(Sadleria)*.
2. Tahiti; also a mythical foreign place, home of many gods.
3. An island in the South Pacific, northwest of Tahiti.
4. One of the four principal Hawaiian gods, god of life and light.

Puʻuʻoniʻoni
Tremble Hill

These words are from an ancient chant attributed to Kamapuaʻa,[1] hog demigod of Kaliuwaʻa (Sacred Falls, Oʻahu), when he went to visit Pele on Hawaiʻi. Abraham Fornander, eminent scholar of Hawaiian literature, gives the following account: The Hiʻiaka sisters[2] of Pele were gathered in the pit of Halemaʻumaʻu Crater. They were stringing *lei* and heard Kamapuaʻa chanting, taunting Pele, from above, on the ridge of ʻAkanikōlea.[3] Nathaniel Emerson, also a noted scholar of Hawaiian literature, preserved another account of this chant.[4] In his version, Hiʻiakaikapoliopele, Pele's youngest and most beloved sister, chanted this poem as she began her journey to Kauaʻi to fetch Pele's lover Lohiʻau. How thrilling to imagine seeing Hiʻiakaikapoliopele and hearing her voice intermingled with bird songs—for she was a child of nature and loved to sing with the forest birds.

Chant type:	Inoa (name)
Chant style:	Mailani (sweet praise)
Hula type:	Noho (seated), ʻIliʻili (pebbles)

1. Said to have once married Pele but later despised by her.
2. Many of Pele's younger sisters carry the name Hiʻiaka, each with a descriptive qualifier at the end that sets her apart from the others, for example, Hiʻiakaiikaʻaleleʻī, Hiʻiaka-in-the-giant-billow. Opinions vary as to exactly how many there are; some sources say eleven.
3. Lit., plover cry; land near Kīlauea Crater.
4. In *Pele and Hiʻiaka, a Myth from Hawaii* (reprint, Rutland, Vt.: Charles E. Tuttle, 1978), p. 20.

Kāhea
> Kumu: "Hoʻomākaukau"
> Haumāna: " ʻAe, a ka luna o Puʻuʻoniʻoni"

A ka luna o Puʻuʻoniʻoni[5]	High above at Puʻuʻoniʻoni
Ke anaina a ka wahine	The goddesses attending Pele have assembled
Kiʻei kaiāulu o Wahinekapu[6]	The community of Wahinekapu peering
Noho ana ʻo Papalauahi[7]	Beyond it lies Papalauahi
Lauahi Pele i kai o Puna	The fires of Pele consume the coast of Puna
One ʻā kai o Malama[8]	Creating cinder heaps at Malama
Mālama i ke kanaka	Take care of your people
A he pua laha ʻole	For they are the rarest of flowers
Haʻina mai ka inoa	The name is declared
Kua kapu o Hiʻiaka	Sacred back [of] Hiʻiaka
"HE INOA NO HIʻIAKAIKAPOLIOPELE"	"A name chant for Hiʻiaka-in-the-bosom-of-Pele"

---

5. Lit., tremble hill; at ʻAkanikōlea, Kīlauea. Kīlauea is an active volcano; eruptions and lava flow cause frequent earth movements in the area.
6. Lit., sacred woman (Pele); a bluff near Kīlauea, taboo residence of the god Kamohoaliʻi, brother of Pele.
7. Southeast Hawaiʻi land section.
8. Inland crater, sea area and land section in Kalapana, Puna district.

Ke Pohā Nei
It Is Rustling

This was performed as a game as well as a light-hearted *hula*. We would imagine Lohiʻau, high chief of Hāʻena[1] and legendary suitor of both Pele and Hiʻiaka, in all his regal splendor playing this game with friends. The sound of whirring tops, fashioned from the lower pointed portion of a coconut shell, ended the dance as all the players fell to their knees in laughter and frivolity. The person whose top or *ʻōniu* spun the longest won the game and the accolades of the group. *Kilu* was another game that involved spinning coconuts. It enjoyed great popularity among the Hawaiians of old, royalty and commoners alike. Both games were competitive and winners would often claim romantic favors as their prize. For this reason Pele, a goddess of fiery passions, is associated with this *hula ʻōniu* as well as with the game of *kilu*.[2]

We included this chant in our 1948–1949 mainland and Mexico concert tour. Brother Keola and cousin Mahi taunted the girls and tried to outdo their spinning skills with comic facial expressions and derisive calls. It was a light moment in the concert and a resounding success. At Carnegie Hall in New York City the late Pearl Buck, renowned author and friend of Sweetheart Grandma, was so captivated she came backstage after the number and whispered loudly to me from the wings, "Charming, utterly charming."

Chant type: Pāʻani (play)
Chant style: ʻOliʻoli (joyous)
Hula type: ʻŌniu (spinning top)

---

1. Lit., red hot; land section and village in the Hanalei district, northwestern Kauaʻi.
2. Personal communication, Frank Werther, Kauaʻi, January 1995.

Kāhea
    Kumu: "Hoʻomākaukau"
    Haumāna: "ʻAe, ke pohā nei ʻuʻina lā"

Ke pohā nei ʻuʻina lā	The whirring and rustling of the spinning top
Kani ʻolēʻolē hauwalaʻau	The sounds of chatter and gossip
Ke wawā Puʻuhinahina[3]	Should Puʻuhinahina make a sound
Kani ka ʻaka	Laughter rings out
Hehene[4] nā pali	Teasing voices [are heard] in the cliffs
Nā pali o Kaiwikuʻi[5]	The cliffs of Kaiwikuʻi
Hanohano Makana[6] i ka Waiʻōpua[7]	Majestic is Makana in the Waiʻōpua wind
Malihini ka hale ua hiki mai	The visitor has arrived at the house
Kani ka pahu a Lohiʻau	The sacred drum of Lohiʻau sounds forth
A Lohiʻau ipo i Hāʻena lā	Lohiʻau the sweetheart chief of Hāʻena
ʻEnaʻena ke aloha ua hiki mai	Love burns brightly upon the arrival [of the visitor]
ʻAuʻau i ka wai a Kanaloa[8]	Bathe in the waters of Kanaloa
Nānā kāua ia Limahuli[9]	Let us [two] look towards Limahuli
E huli ʻoe a loaʻa pono	Seek out the way to win
Kā ia nei ʻōniu	This person's spinning top
"HE INOA NO LOHIʻAU"	"A name chant for Lohiʻau"

---

3. Meaning the top falls over. Refers to a precipitous place on the coast near Hāʻena (Nathaniel B. Emerson, *Unwritten Literature of Hawaii: The Sacred Songs of the Hula* [reprint, Rutland, Vt.: Charles E. Tuttle, 1965], p. 248).
4. Word used by Sweetheart Grandma when chanting this *mele*; probably the colloquial version of *"henehene,"* as *"mamake"* is to *"makemake."*
5. High cliffs against which the waves dash (Emerson, *Unwritten Literature,* p. 248).
6. Lit., gift; cliff in Hāʻena where Lohiʻau was entombed.
7. Name of a pleasant breeze.
8. Lit., the waters of Kanaloa; Kanaloa was one of the great Hawaiian gods, called a god of healing. Also the name of a wet cave in Hāʻena.
9. Lit., the turning or searching hand; falls, stream and valley near Hāʻena; also the name of the wind of Hāʻena.

ʻOaka Ē Ka Lani
The Heavens Flash

My first recollection of this *hula Pele* was an exciting performance by my aunt, Harriett Beamer (Magoon). She was a strikingly beautiful woman, Papa's sister. Her carriage was erect and aloof. With great dramatic quality and piercing expression, she personified Madame Pele herself. I had never seen a *hula* performed in this manner. I was later to see ʻIolani Luahine dance this and, again, the character personified was remarkable. Of course, both dancers were acting out the story, their own personalities subdued by Pele. "Bombastic" seems a mild word for the thrilling action of hands clapping, feet stamping, body writhing, head and long flowing hair thrown about in wild abandon. The contrast of respect interrupts the flow of energy as the dancer ritards the entire action, tempo and pulse in *"ʻEliʻeli kau mai"* (May a deep respect come to us). Then the tempo resumes with a fury. I have always believed that this would be one of the few chants brought to life more fully with the sound of the dancer's own voice calling out the words throughout as she lived through the actions.

Chant type: Hoʻomaikaʻi (praise)
Chant style: Kūō (bombastic)
Hula type: Pele (volcano goddess)

Kāhea
    Kumu: "Hoʻomākaukau"
    Haumāna: "ʻAe, lapakū ka wahine aʻo Pele i Kahiki"

Lapakū ka wahine aʻo Pele i Kahiki[1]	The woman Pele abounds with energy and activity in Kahiki
ʻOaka ē ka lani noke nō	The heavens flash on and on
ʻOaka ē ka lani noke nō	The heavens flash on and on
ʻEliʻeli kau mai	May a deep respect come to us
ʻEliʻeli kau mai	May a deep respect come to us
ʻOaka ē ka lani noke nō	The heavens flash on and on
ʻOaka ē ka lani noke nō	The heavens flash on and on
Ūhīʻūhā mai ana ʻo Pele	The raging of Pele can be heard
I ka lua aʻo Halemaʻumaʻu	In the pit of Halemaʻumaʻu
ʻOaka ē ka lani noke nō	The heavens flash on and on
ʻOaka ē ka lani noke nō	The heavens flash on and on
E Pele	O Pele
E Pele ē	O Pele
"HE INOA NO PELE"	"In the name of Pele"

1. Tahiti; any foreign land; a mythical homeland of many gods.

Nā Aliʻi
The Chiefs

Countless chants and songs were written for and dedicated to those who ruled Hawaiian society. There were numerous classes and ranks of aliʻi, *the aristocrats who were chiefs and chiefesses, kings and queens. The* aliʻi maoli *were true chiefs, while the* aliʻi kuʻi *might be thought of as supplemental kings, powers behind the throne. The* aliʻi pūʻō lani *were exalted chiefs, the* kūʻokoʻa *independent chiefs. The list goes on ... aliʻi papa, aliʻi poʻe kauā and other lesser chiefs. The* aliʻi kāne *were male chiefs and the* aliʻi wahine *female chiefesses. As the chants are studied, teachers and students will want to learn more about the* aliʻi *mentioned. We are thankful for the many wonderful books that have been written on this subject, by scholars of times gone by and those of recent years.*

E Manono
O Manono

Princess Manono was one of our ancestors. The name is used today among several family members including me, Kapuailohiamanonokalani (The-precious-flower-of-the-great-Chiefess Manono).

The Battle of Kuamoʻo[1] in 1819 is well documented. The defenders of the ancient Hawaiian religion made a valiant stand against those, including the king, Kamehameha II,[2] who favored breaking the sacred laws that had governed the people of Hawaiʻi for hundreds of years. Manono is cited as a brave woman, wife of High Chief Kekuaokalani (The-god-of-the-heavens) of Kona, Hawaiʻi island. Kekuaokalani was a cousin of Liholiho, Kamehameha II, and he played a significant role as caretaker of the ancient Hawaiian gods. He was fiercely opposed to Liholiho's lifting of the *kapu* (sacred prohibitions). As the story was passed down in the family and told to me by Sweetheart Grandma, Manono, like her husband, felt strongly about keeping the old ways and begged her husband to let her take part in the battle. She vehemently opposed the burning of the old temples and the destruction of the ancient god images to make way for the new religion. Manono and Kekuaokalani were a loving couple, deeply devoted to each other. As it was not custom for a chiefess to take part in battle, Kekuaokalani promised to fix a *hāliʻi pūnana* (smooth nest) of *uluhe* ferns[3] from which Manono could safely observe the action on the battlefield.

The forces of Liholiho, armed with muskets and cannons inherited from his father, soon defeated the forces of Kekuaokalani. When Manono saw her husband fall she ran to him, covered his face with his feathered cape and, picking up his spear, plunged into the heat of the battle crying out, "*Kō aloha, mālama kō aloha*" (Your love, keep your love). The conservative forces rallied for a brief time but soon Manono too was killed.

The story unfolds further. The captured troops were held in a Kona stockade. All during the long, dark night their chanting filled the air. At dawn, Liholiho came to the stockade and heard the love chant of Manono. With the final words of Manono ringing clearly, Liholiho was touched and his heart softened. He threw open the stockade gates and pardoned all the prisoners to return to their homes. This was the last major battle fought in Hawaiʻi. In our family, the plea of Manono is revered: "*Kō aloha, mālama kō aloha*."

Chant type: Hoʻoipoipo (romantic)
Chant style: Hoʻoipo (personal love)
Hula type: Pā Ipu (hand gourd drum), ʻŌlapa (standing, moving)

Kāhea	Kumu:	"Hoʻomākaukau"
	Haumāna:	"ʻAe, e Manono lā"

E Manono lā ʻeā	O Manono tra la
E Manono lā ʻeā	O Manono tra la
ʻAe ʻoe ʻae ʻoe ē	La la la la
Kau ka ʻopeʻope	Place the bundles [of love]
Ka ulu hala lā ʻeā	In the pandanus grove tra la
ʻAe ʻoe ʻae ʻoe ē	La la la la
Ka uluhe lā ʻeā	The wild staghorn fern tra la
Ka uluhe lā ʻeā	The wild staghorn fern tra la
ʻAe ʻoe ʻae ʻoe ē	La la la la
Hāliʻi pūnana	A nest is spread
No huli mai	Now turn to me
ʻAe ʻoe ʻae ʻoe ē	La la la la
Huli mai ʻoe lā	Turn to me now
Moe kāua	Let us rest
ʻAe ʻoe ʻae ʻoe ē	La la la la
Hāliʻi pūnana	A nest is spread
No huli mai	Now turn to me
ʻAe ʻoe ʻae ʻoe ē	La la la la
E Manono lā ʻeā	O Manono tra la
E Manono lā ʻeā	O Manono tra la
ʻAe ʻoe ʻae ʻoe ē	La la la la
Kau ka ʻopeʻope	Put down the bundles
Ka ulu hala lā ʻeā	In the pandanus grove tra la
ʻAe ʻoe ʻae ʻoe ē	La la la la
Kō aloha lā ʻeā	Your love tra la
Kō aloha lā ʻeā	Your love tra la
ʻAe ʻoe ʻae ʻoe ē	La la la la
Mālama kō aloha	Keep your love
Mālama kō aloha	Keep your love
ʻAe ʻoe ʻae ʻoe ē	La la la la
Mālama kō aloha	Keep your love
"HE INOA NO MANONO"	"A name chant for Manono"

1. Lit., backbone; land section in Kailua, Kona, on the leeward side of Hawaiʻi island.
2. Oldest son of Kamehameha the Great, who became king on his father's death in 1819. He journeyed to England and died there on July 14, 1824. Also named Kalaninuikualiholihoikekapu (The-great-chief-[with the]-burning-back-taboo), referring to the taboo against approaching Liholiho (lit., glowing) from the back.
3. Hawaiian species of false staghorn fern (three genera).

Moe Aku
Asleep [Are We]

Sweetheart Grandma loved Queen Emma[1] (1836–1885) for her many fine qualities. When she taught us name chants for the queen, Grandma embellished the poetry with many colorful descriptions, constantly reminding us of Emma's dignified stature and strong character. As a child, the images in my mind of this outing with Queen Emma were vivid. I could smell the damp forest and feel the cool air on my skin. Picturing the colorful land shells and imagining their trilling continues to intrigue me to this day.

The chant files of the Kamehameha Schools tell the background of this chant: "This mele was composed in 1871 commemorating the mountain hike of about a hundred people, including hula girls, retainers, musicians and children that were stretched along the Kaua'i trail for nearly half a mile. They went single file through the rough terrain and fog-chilled forests. There were empty areas where a misstep would make a person sink waist-deep in mud. A night was spent in 'Aipō-nui[2] forest, at a place called Waineki.[3] The next day was spent hiking the rest of the trail to the Kilohana,[4] or look-out, of Hanalei."[5]

Chant type: Inoa (name)
Chant style: Mailani (sweet praise)
Hula type: Ho'onānā (soothing, quiet), Noho (seated)

Kāhea
    Kumu: "Ho'omākaukau"
    Haumāna: " 'Ae, moe aku i ka hale 'ama'u"

Moe aku i ka hale 'ama'u[6]	Asleep [are we] in the shelter of the tree fern
Hale o ka pūpū-kani-oe[7]	House of the land shell
A he 'ehu wāwae 'elekini	The footprints grow faint
Kinikini nā hoa pa'iniu[8]	Many are the friends amidst the *pa'iniu*

1. Wife of Alexander Liholiho, King Kamehameha IV. After her son's and husband's deaths, Queen Emma continued to play an important role in the political activities of her nation.
2. Lit., big [larger in area] eating by dark; summit swamp on Kaua'i's highest mountain, Wai'ale'ale.
3. Lit., bulrush water; swampy mountains above Waimea town, Kaua'i.
4. Peak and crater in Kaua'i's Līhu'e district.
5. District on Kaua'i's North Shore.
6. A genus of ferns with trunks, found only in Hawai'i (*Sadleria* spp.). In Sweetheart Grandma's ledger, the words "*hale 'āmala*" were used. This would refer to a blacksmith's shop, but the true hidden meaning of this line as such is unclear. She taught me to use "*hale 'ama'u*"; I suspect this was due to my young age.
7. Lit., shell that sounds long; a land shell (snail) *(Partulina physa)*.
8. Native Hawaiian lilies *(Astelid* spp.*)*.

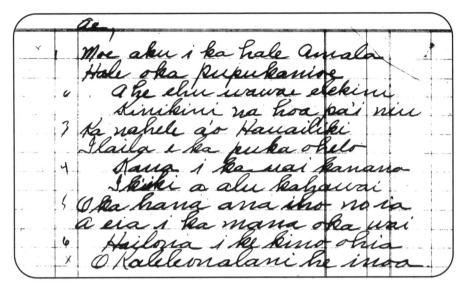

Excerpt from "Moe Aku" as written down by Sweetheart Grandma (see Introduction).

Ka nahele a'o Haua'iliki[9]	There in the forest of Haua'iliki
I laila ē ka puka 'ōhelo[10]	At the entrance where the *'ōhelo* berries blossom
Ka ua i Kauaikanānā[11]	The rain falls high up at Kauaikanānā
Ikiiki a 'alu kahawai	Weary by the river ravine
'O ka hana 'ana iho nō ia	This is the work to be done
A eia i ka mana o ka wai	Here where the stream divides and branches out
Hailona i ke kino 'ōhi'a[12]	A symbol of the strong and sacred one
'O Kaleleonālani[13] he inoa	Queen Emma is her name
He paia 'ala i ke anu	The forest clearing is fragrant in the cold
He nohea i ka wao nahele	Lovely in the woodlands
Kūpaoa i ke 'ala	So very fragrant is the scent
Ke 'ala o ka hinahina[14]	The fragrance of the *hinahina*
"HE INOA NO EMALANI"	"A name chant for Queen Emma"

9. Lit., bitter cold; name of place in the Alaka'i Swamp, on Kaua'i.
10. A small native shrub *(Vaccinium reticulatum)* in the cranberry family.
11. A stream and valley on the Nāpali Coast of Kaua'i.
12. A tree, common in wet areas *(Metrosideros macropus, M. collina* subsp. *polymorpha).* Sometimes used in Hawaiian poetry to show high rank or stature.
13. The-flight-of-the-heavenly-ones; Hawaiian name of Queen Emma, taken in 1863 after the deaths of her child, Ka Haku O Hawai'i, and her husband, Kamehameha IV (Alexander Liholiho).
14. Silvery native geranium *(Geranium cuneatum).*

He Wahine Holo Lio
A Horsewoman

Emma Rooke (Emalani Kaleleonālani)[1] was fond of horseback riding on her favorite chestnut stallion, Kīna'u.[2] This version of a well-known mele is unlike any other I have seen. It is from Grandma's ledger, word for word as she wrote it down. Isn't it wonderful to have variant words, variant verses and different thoughts interjected in chants we have long made a part of our lives? I wrote a melody for this chant in 1950 after dancing it for twenty years. I combined chant with alternating verses of melody. It was a new concept for those early years.

Since the early 1800s, Hawaiian women have been a part of celebratory pageantry as they developed riding skills, invented long glorious *pā'ū* (skirts) and became horsewomen of note. Aunty Mona Hind of Pu'uwa'awa'a Ranch, Hawai'i island, was one of the finest horsewomen I knew. When Sweetheart Grandma took me to the Hind ranch, I reveled in Aunty Mona's regal figure on horseback. Later Papa took me to meet Anna Perry-Fiske at Anna Ranch in Waimea, another great Hawai'i island horsewoman. When I rode at the Beamer Ranch, I had many role models to emulate—beginning with Queen Emma.

Chant type:	Inoa (name)
Chant style:	'Oli'oli (joyous), Mailani (sweet praise)
Hula type:	Holo Lio (horseback riding), 'Ōlapa (standing, moving)

---

1. Lit., Flight-of-the-heavenly-ones; a name taken by Queen Emma after the deaths of her son, Prince Albert, in 1862 and of her husband, Kamehameha IV, in 1863.
2. Also the name of her mother-in-law.

Kāhea
        Kumu: "Hoʻomākaukau"
        Haumāna: "ʻAe, he wahine holo lio"

He wahine holo lio ʻoe ā	You are quite a horsewoman
Kōwelo ana kō hae	With your ribbons streaming like a flag
Kohukohu maoli ʻoe ā	You are such a beautiful sight
Ma luna o Kīnaʻu lio	Sitting upon your horse Kīnaʻu
Ka lio hula haole ā	The horse does a foreign dance
Pau nā holo ʻelua	Mastering the two-step
I ke kula ʻo Kaukeano[3] ā	On the plains of Kaukeano
Anoano mai ke aloha	Feelings of love for you overwhelm me
E aloha aʻe ana au ā	My love goes
I ka pua lā o ka hau[4]	To the blossom of the *hau* tree
Hoʻokahi nō hāuna ā	There is only one enticement
Leha wale mai ʻo ia la	As that one furtively glances my way
ʻO ia la nō kuʻu hoa ā	That one is my sweet friend
E pupue ma ke kūʻono	Crouching there in the corner
ʻĀpuka maoli ʻoe ā	You are deceiving yourself
I ka nui o kuʻu pono	About the true nature of my character
Aia nō kō hiki mai ā	You are just arriving to be with me
I ka welo ʻana o ka lā	As the sun slowly sets at the end of the day
Kuene pono iho au ā	I have arranged everything as best can be
I paʻa pono ke kahua	The foundation is firm and solid
He inoa hoʻohiehie ā	A name song in praise of one who is so dignified
No Kaleleonālani	For Kaleleonālani

"HE INOA NO EMALANI"   "A name chant for Queen Emma"

---

3. Lit., awe inspiring; area at Beretania and Richards Streets in Honolulu where the first Central Union Church was built.
4. A lowland tree *(Hibiscus tiliaceus)* with yellow-red, cup-shaped flowers.

Kau Iī Lua
Doubly Chilled

This chant was originally dedicated to Kaumealani (Kameali'i), a high-ranking chiefess of Waialua, O'ahu, daughter of the chant's composer, Kapela, and a relative of King Kalākaua.[1] Its poetry is particularly illusive and obscure, which may account for the variety of translations used by *hula* devotees. This version is based on several translations by Mary Kawena Pūku'i, one by Ka'upena Wong also based on the work of Pūku'i, translation and discussion with Pōhaku Nishimitsu, and our own experiences in performing and studying this *mele*. The serious student of *hula* is referred to in-depth analyses by Adrienne Kaeppler and Elizabeth Tatar.[2] Because of the chant's exceptional philosophical content, the dance is always performed with dignity and reverence. It has indeed become a classic in *hula* literature.

Chant type: Ho'omaika'i (praise), 'Āina (land)
Chant style: Mailani (sweet praise)
Hula type: Pahu (drum), 'Ōlapa (standing, moving)

Kāhea

    Kumu: "Ho'omākaukau"
    Haumāna: "'Ae, kau lī lua i ke anu Wai'ale'ale"

---

1. Kaulīlua is another name for the last king of Hawai'i, David Kalākaua, who ruled from 1874 to 1891. He was noted for being the first of the world's monarchs to travel around the world, for having created 'Iolani Palace and for his dedication to Hawaiian culture.
2. In *Hula Pahu: Hawaiian Drum Dances,* vol. 1, *Ha'a and Hula Pahu: Sacred Movements,* and vol. 2, *The Pahu: Sounds of Power* (Honolulu: Bishop Museum Press, 1993).

Kau lī lua i ke anu Waiʻaleʻale[3]	A doubly bitter chill settles on Waiʻaleʻale
He maka hālalo ka lehua maka noe[4]	The centers of the *lehua maka noe* are overturned
He lihilihi kukū ia no ʻAipō[5]	Like a thorny lace surrounding the swamp of ʻAipō
ʻO ka hulu ʻāʻā ia aʻo Hauaʻiliki[6]	Like small feathers adorning Hauaʻiliki
Ua pehi ʻia e ka ua a ʻeha ka nahele	Pelted by the rain the forest suffers
Māui ka pua uē i ke anu	Bruised is the flower crying in the cold
I ke kukuna lā wai o mokihana[7]	The rays of the sun shine through the mist of the *mokihana*
Ua hana ʻia e ka pono a ua pololei	What is correct and just has been done
Ua haʻina ʻia aku nō iā ʻoe	Indeed it has been told to you
ʻO ke ola nō ia aʻo kiaʻi loko	It is the very life of the guardian of the pond
Kiʻei i Kaʻula[8] nānā i ka makani	Peer at Kaʻula watch every breeze
Hoʻolono ka leo ka halulu o ka Māluakele[9]	Listen to the voice the roar of the Māluakele wind
Kiʻei hālō i Makaʻikeʻole[10]	Peering and peeping at Makaʻikeʻole
Kāmau ke ea ka Hālauāola[11]	The breath of life continues at Hālauāola
He kula lima ia no Wāwaenohu[12]	Wāwaenohu is a plain that invites a fond caress
Me he pūkoʻa hakahaka lā i Waʻahila[13]	Like coral fissured by the Waʻahila rain
Ka momoku a ka unu Unulau o Lehua[14]	Broken by the stirrings of the Unulau wind of Lehua
A lehulehu ka hale pono	When there are many at home
Leʻa ka haʻawina	Giving is a pleasure
Ke ʻala mai nei ʻo ka puka o ka hale	A fragrance lingers at the door of the house
E ō ē	Answer the call

"HE INOA NO KALĀKAUA"   "A name chant for Kalākaua"

---

3. Lit., rippling water; highest mountain on Kauaʻi.
4. Lit., *lehua* with misty face; a small shrub *(Metrosideros pumila)* found only on Kauaʻi.
5. Summit swamp on Waiʻaleʻale.
6. Lit., bitter cold; place name on Kauaʻi in the Alakaʻi Swamp.
7. Native tree of the citrus family with an anise-scented berry *(Pelea anisata)*, found only on Kauaʻi; also an area in Kōkeʻe, Kauaʻi.
8. Lit., the redness; rocky islet southwest of Niʻihau.
9. Lit., damp Mālua; trade wind of north Kauaʻi.
10. Lit., eyes that do not see; area around the summit of Waiʻaleʻale.
11. Lit., [the] longhouse of [Chief] Ola; area in Kōkeʻe, also called Kahālauaola.
12. Place in Kōkeʻe; also a red cloud seen in the western sky at sunset from Mānā.
13. Name of a Mānoa rain; also an area in Mānoa; ridge separating Mānoa and Pālolo Valleys.
14. The Unulau wind is famous in song. It can be found on Kauaʻi, West Maui and Niʻihau; here it is attributed to Lehua, an island west of Niʻihau, which is named for the flower.

Aia I Haili Kō Lei Nani
There at Haili Is Your Precious Garland

The famed Kapioʻlani[1] *lei* chants, one for each island, create a wreath of praise expressing love for the queen. This is the one that concerns places on Hawaiʻi island. Sweetheart Grandma revered chants of "her" island of Hawaiʻi and taught them to us with great spirituality and love. In addition, Grandma and her family were all staunch members of historic Haili Congregational Church[2] in Hilo. Her uncle, the Reverend Stephen Desha, was the beloved pastor there for many years. She herself was organist and choir director. For reasons of devotion and loyalty, I think she favored this chant with special love.

Chant type: Kūō (praise)
Chant style: Mailani (sweet praise)
Hula type: ʻŌlapa (standing, moving)

From Sweetheart Grandma's ledger, under the title "Kapiʻolani," we find a good example of how these chants were written without being divided into verses. Note also that some of the spelling conventions have changed through time, most notably the use of diacritics.

Kāhea
> Kumu: "Hoʻomākaukau"
> Haumāna: " ʻAe, aia i Haili kō lei nani"

Aia i Haili[3] kō lei nani	There at Haili is your precious garland
I ka nuʻa lehua[4] i Mōkaulele[5]	The heaped-up *lehua* at Mōkaulele
ʻO ka pāpahi lei o ka ʻāina	A wreath to adorn the land
I kuia mai e Hilo Hanakahi[6]	Strung by Hilo Hanakahi
Hoʻokahi hoʻi ʻoe hoʻokahi au	You and I are here by ourselves
I ka nahele aloha ʻo Pāʻieʻie[7]	In the beloved forest of Pāʻieʻie
Noho mai ʻo Uēhanokahuna[8]	There sits Uēhanokahuna
Ka uahi noe o Kīlauea[9]	The smoky mist of Kīlauea
ʻUpu aʻe ka manaʻo liʻa i ka nani	Thoughts come to mind entranced in the beauty
I ka papa lohi lua aʻo Maukele[10]	In the doubly sparkling plains of Maukele
ʻO ka lohi mai kāu e Wahinekapu[11]	You are sparkling there Wahinekapu
Eia aʻe ka makani a he Puʻulena[12]	Here comes the Puʻulena wind
Nāna i kui lima mai i ka nahele	She who took the forest by hand
I like aku ai me ka nuku o ka manu	So that it became like the beak of a bird
ʻO wai ka i ʻike iā Mauna Kea[13]	Who has seen Mauna Kea
ʻAʻohe ona lua e like ai	There is nothing to compare it with
Haʻina ʻia mai ana ka puana	Let the refrain be told
ʻO Kapiʻolani i ka ʻiu o luna	Kapiʻolani is the most sacred one on high
"HE INOA NO KAPIʻOLANI"	"A name chant for Kapiʻolani"

1. Royal chiefess (b. 1834, d. 1899); wife of Kalākaua; granddaughter of Kaumualiʻi, last king of independent Kauaʻi.
2. So named because the timber to build the original church came from nearby Haili Forest.
3. Lit., loving memory; forest area near Hilo.
4. The official flower of Hawaiʻi island.
5. Place near Haili.
6. An ancient Hilo chief.
7. Lit., ʻieʻie vine enclosure; land near Panaʻewa, south of Hilo.
8. Cliff at Kīlauea Crater.
9. Active volcano on the flank of Mauna Loa.
10. Place name at Puna.
11. A bluff near Kīlauea Crater.
12. A famous cold wind of Kīlauea and Puna.
13. Mountain in the Kōhala district, highest in all of the Hawaiian Islands.

I Aloha I Kō A Ka Wai
How Loving When Pulled by the Current

There is a paucity of chants composed for Prince Kalaniana'ole.[1] I have loved this one with increasing tenderness over the years. The love poetry appeals to my femininity and its innocence touches my heart. Princess Elizabeth Kahanu, wife of Prince Kalaniana'ole, was my grandmother's cousin. Sweetheart Grandma composed lovely songs for Princess Kahanu, a family favorite being "Ke Ali'i Hulu Mamo." Because of the special love between the two cousins, a precious rapport existed and found expression in the Kūhiō Kalaniana'ole chants and songs that we performed with great pride. I transferred Grandma's, Mother's and Papa's love of Kūhiō to my own life, remembering many family stories about this favorite prince. Granduncle Judge Jack Desha was secretary to Prince Kūhiō and we had letters from the prince asking to play baseball with "Uncle" Jack and his brother, "Uncle" Stephen Desha Jr., at Mo'oheau Park in Hilo. When the prince died, in 1922, the Kamehameha Schools cadets accompanied the casket from Kawaiaha'o Church to the Royal Mausoleum, Mauna'ala, in Nu'uanu, O'ahu. Papa was one of those cadets and was given a small *koa*[2] wood heart, about two inches in diameter, as a keepsake. These *koa* hearts had been crafted to adorn the outside of the casket. Papa gave me the heart to remind me of our *ali'i*—and to this day I treasure it. Although this chant was composed to honor Kalaniana'ole, Sweetheart Grandma taught it to us with the dedication to his mother, Kinoiki.[3]

Chant type:	Inoa (name)
Chant style:	'Oli'oli (joyous), Ho'oipo (personal love)
Hula type:	Ku'i (interpretive), 'Ōlapa (standing, moving)

---

1. Jonah Kūhiō Kalaniana'ole (1871-1922), Hawai'i's delegate to the U.S. Congress and father of the Hawaiian Homes Commission Act. He was the nephew and adopted son of King Kalākaua and his wife, Queen Kapi'olani.
2. The largest of native forest trees *(Acacia koa)*.
3. Sister of Kapi'olani (wife of Kalākaua); mother of Kalaniana'ole, Edward Keli'iahonui and David Kawānanakoa.

Kāhea
    Kumu: "Hoʻomākaukau"
    Haumāna: " 'Ae, i aloha i kō a ka wai"

I aloha i kō a ka wai lā	How loving when pulled by the current
I kaʻi mai anu kou ala	As you come towards me cold is your path
Ua anu nā pua o ka laina lā	The descendants of the line are cold
Ka wahine noho anu o ke kula lā	The woman dwells on the cold plain
A luna au aʻo Poliʻahu[4] lā	I was up at Poliʻahu
Ahuwale kai aʻo Wailua[5] lā	I could easily view the sea at Wailua
Lua ʻole ka hana a ka makani lā	The force of the wind is unequaled
A ke Kiukeʻe[6] aʻo nā pali lā	The Kiukeʻe wind of the cliffs
Pā iho ke kai aʻo Puna[7] lā	The sea of Puna strikes [the cliffs]
Ko Puna meaʻ maʻa mau ia lā	Puna is accustomed to that
Pau ai koʻu lihi hoihoi lā	Finished completely is my interest
I ka wai ʻāwili me ke kai lā	In this place where stream meets the sea
Ke ʻono hou nei kuʻu puʻu lā	My throat thirsts to taste once more
I ka wai huʻihuʻi o ka uka lā	The cold waters of the uplands
Wai hone i ke kumu o nā pali lā	Murmuring waters at the base of the cliff
I ka malu i ka lau kukui lā	In the shade of the candlenut tree
Ke kuhi nei au a he pono lā	I think it is right
Ka ʻilima[8] lei a ke aloha lā	That the ʻilima be made into a garland of love
Āu i kau nui aku ai lā	It is that which you have worn so often
I ka nani ʻoi aʻo ia pua lā	It is the most beautiful of flowers
Haʻina ʻia mai ana ka puana lā	Tell the refrain
No Kinoiki nō kuʻu mele lā	My song is for Kinoiki
"HE INOA NO KINOIKI"	"A name chant for Kinoiki"

4. Lit., garment [for the] bosom; *heiau* in Wailua, Kauaʻi.
5. Valley and town near Līhuʻe, Kauaʻi.
6. Name of wind of Nāwiliwili, Kauaʻi.
7. District of eastern Kauaʻi, also called Kawaihau.
8. Native shrub bearing tiny yellow-red flowers (*Sida* spp.); the flower of Oʻahu.

Lanakila
Victory

This chant tells of a trip Queen Liliʻuokalani[1] took on her train, the "Lanikila" (Victory). The royal train was not only famous but loved like a person, perhaps because the train was honored by carrying the royal personage of Hawaiʻi's last queen. It was not uncommon in Hawaiian thinking to recognize "life" in inanimate objects, treating them in a loving fashion and often giving them names. At each stop of the royal tour, the people gathered in great throngs to pay homage to their beloved *aliʻi*.

Chant type: Inoa (name)
Chant style: ʻOliʻoli (joyous)
Hula type: ʻUlīʻulī (gourd rattle)

---

1. Older sister of King Kalākaua; queen of Hawaiʻi from 1891 to 1893.

Kāhea

    Kumu: "Hoʻomākaukau"
    Haumāna: "ʻAe, ʻo Lanakila ke kaʻaahi aliʻi"

ʻO Lanakila ke kaʻaahi aliʻi	Lanakila was the royal train
Nāna i lawe mai kahu aupuni	That carried the protector of the realm
A hiki ʻo Kalani i Moanalua[2]	The princess arrived at Moanalua
Ka uapo holuholu aʻo Hālawa[3]	At the swaying bridge of Hālawa
ʻAlawa iho ʻoe ma ka ʻao ʻao	A glance over the sides showed
Ke nome ka huila i ke alahao	The wheels rolling persistently along the tracks
ʻAʻohe ou loa aʻe Mānana[4]	Mānana did not seem far
I ke kuʻupau a nā mikini	As the engines worked with all their power
Hoʻokahi nō leo aʻo ke kuhina	The officer spoke just once
Hoʻopaʻa ʻia mai nā mikini	Bring the engines to a halt
Kūnou welo pāpale ke aloha	Bowing and waving hats with love
Nā kupa nā kini ou e Kalani	The multitudes the natives are yours O heavenly one
A kau ʻo Kalani i ke kaʻa piʻo	The princess boarded her carriage
Huli aku huli mai hoʻolaʻilaʻi	Enjoying herself turning this way and that
Kiani ka uepa haʻa nā lio	The whip snapped and the horses pranced
Kiliʻopu i ke kula o Leilehua[5]	Gracefully over the plains of Leilehua
Hea aku mākou ō mai ʻoe	We call to you, answer us
ʻO Liliʻuokalani lā he inoa ʻae	Liliʻuokalani is your name indeed
Haʻina ʻia mai ana ka puana	Tell the refrain of the story
He inoa no Liliʻu kahu aupuni	In the name of Liliʻu protector of the realm
"HE INOA NO LILIʻUOKALANI"	"A name chant for Liliʻuokalani"

---

2. Land division near Fort Shafter, Honolulu.
3. Land section and stream at Waipahu, Oʻahu.
4. Land division and stream at Pearl City, Oʻahu.
5. Plains near Wahiawā, Oʻahu.

No Ke Ano Ahiahi
In the Evening Time

Dating from the mid-1800s, this melodic chant mentions sailing ships and the land of America. The sweet, plaintive melody infuses the feelings of parting with a loving tenderness. It is dedicated to Lunalilo, affectionately known as Prince Bill before his ascension to the throne as the king of Hawai'i. Though King Lunalilo's reign was a scant year (1873–1874), it was an illustrious period of Hawai'i's history. Prince William Lunalilo was elected king by the vote of the legislature. This was a new concept in Hawaiian politics and government. To let the people have a voice in choosing the king was an exciting turn of events. Also during these years, many Hawaiians ventured abroad. Hawaiians were panning for gold in California, settling in Utah because of religious beliefs and traveling around the world as seamen. A seafaring people with sailing skills, Hawaiians were in great demand aboard ships.

Chant type: Inoa (name)
Chant style: Mailani (sweet praise)
Hula type: Pū'ili (bamboo rattle), Noho (seated)

Kāhea   Kumu: "Ho'omākaukau"
         Haumāna: " 'Ae, no ke ano ahiahi ke aloha"

No ke ano ahiahi ke aloha lā　　　　　　　　In the evening hours we feel *aloha*
I ka hāli'ali'a 'ana mai　　　　　　　　　　Fond memories return

'O ko'u lā heo kēia lā　　　　　　　　　　　This is my day of departure
Ke lū mai nei nā pe'a　　　　　　　　　　　The sails are being unfurled

Ke hiu nei ka heleuma lā　　　　　　　　　　The anchor is hauled up
Ua kau ē ka hae ma hope　　　　　　　　　　The flag is at the stern

Huli a'e 'oe a hele kāua lā　　　　　　　　Turn about and let us [two] go
Eia i ka moana lipolipo　　　　　　　　　　Here we find ourselves in the deep blue sea

Kau aku kāua a ho'i lā　　　　　　　　　　　Let the two of us return
E 'ike iā Amaleka 'ailana　　　　　　　　　To see the island of America

Ha'ina kou inoa e ke ali'i lā　　　　　　　This is the praise of the chief
No ka lani Lunalilo he inoa　　　　　　　　For the chief Lunalilo a name chant

"HE INOA NO LUNALILO"　　　　　　　　　　　"A name chant for Lunalilo"

He Maʻi No Kalani
A Personal Chant for the Chief

Mele celebrating procreative powers are a significant segment of Hawaiian chant literature. These *mele maʻi* (personal chants) were considered of utmost importance in assuring the continuation of the royal line. As I was growing up, it was not part of our family tradition to share *mele maʻi* with the girls. Mother did teach this chant to brother Keola and cousin Mahi, who performed it with great gusto and innocence. I learned my first *mele maʻi* after I was married. Having had wonderful literature classes in college, this sophisticated poetry commanded my deep respect. It contains many levels of meaning that call for philosophical understanding. This chant form is not frivolous or casual poetry, although it is performed with abandon and gaiety. The Hawaiian people are enjoying the revitalization of this art form today. We have erudite scholars like Rubellite Kawena Johnson, illustrious University of Hawaiʻi professor of Hawaiian language, well known for her devotion to Hawaiian literature. Our dear Sarah Nākoa, now deceased, will always be remembered as a kind, loving scholar and source of spiritual guidance who lived an exemplary Hawaiian life. Both these ladies kindly shared their exceptional *mele maʻi* translations with me. We are all grateful to these outstanding scholars for their unstinting generosity.

Chant type: Maʻi (personal)   Chant style: ʻAihaʻa (vigorous)   Hula type: ʻŌlapa (standing, moving)

Kāhea   Kumu: "Hoʻomākaukau"
           Haumāna: "ʻAe, he maʻi no Kalani"

He maʻi no Kalani haʻuhaʻu ē	This is a personal chant for the chief puff puff
No Kahoʻānokū[1] haʻuhaʻu ē	For Kahoʻānokū puff puff
Hoʻolewa aʻe ʻoe haʻuhaʻu ē	Lift your hips puff puff
A i kū pono iho haʻuhaʻu ē	So it stands tall puff puff
Ka pae nā ʻolo haʻuhaʻu ē	A cluster of gourds puff puff
Nā ʻolo o ka puhi haʻuhaʻu ē	The fat of the eel's jaw puff puff
I lalo iho ʻoe haʻuhaʻu ē	Down you go puff puff
A i lalo i ke pulu haʻuhaʻu ē	To rest upon the soft cushion puff puff
Haʻina kō maʻi haʻuhaʻu ē	Tell the refrain of the personal chant puff puff
A he maʻi no Kalani haʻuhaʻu ē	A personal chant for the heavenly one puff puff
"HE MAʻI NO KALANI"	"A personal chant for the Chief"

1. Son of Kamehameha I and Peleuli, born 1785, died 1809. He was the father of Keahikunikekauʻōnohi, a taboo chiefess.

```
        ——— Iolani ———        (For Queen Emma)
He mai keia, ehe, aha
No Iolani            "    "
Aia ko mai           "    "
La i Huilawe         "    "
Ke lawe nei          "    "
No kikala            "    "
E ka laau            "    "
Pahu aka welo        "    "
E ka pahiolo         "    "
Ke olo nei           "    "
Paa ko lima          "    "
E ii nei             "    "
Haina ko mai         "    "
Ke kuini Emma Lani   "    "
——— No Kaleleonalani He Inoa ———
Makai ao Halekauila-la
Ike iu na kumu o ka hana-la
Ehuehu na makainana-la
Pau oe i ke kuhi mai-la
A e ake aku ana ka manao-la
Ai kau ka lii alii nani-la
A e noho Kalele nalani-la
```

This page from Sweetheart Grandma's ledger gives us two chants for Queen Emma Kaleleonālani, the first being what we refer to opposite as "He Ma'i No 'Iolani." The second recalls the riot that occurred at Halekauila and Fort Streets in Honolulu during Queen Emma's and King Kalākaua's election campaign; Sweetheart Grandma put a melody to this chant, which was recorded many years later by Keola and Kapono.

He Maʻi No ʻIolani
A Personal Chant for ʻIolani

This chant is most commonly dedicated to ʻIolani, another name for Alexander Liholiho, Kamehameha IV. This text, however, comes directly from Sweetheart Grandma's ledger, dedicating it to the king's wife, Queen Emma. I never learned this dance. Because of Sweetheart Grandma's upbringing, I suppose she did not consider this "ladylike" material for her granddaughter to study. I knew of it, though, and had seen ʻIolani Luahine dancing it in high spirits. When I asked her, she gave me an honest, forthright interpretation for which I have been grateful all these years. As I have progressed in my research I have come to realize the import and subtle sensitivity of the *maʻi* chants. They are to be treated respectfully and performed with joy and vigor.

Chant type: Maʻi (personal)
Chant style: ʻAihaʻa (vigorous)
Hula type: ʻŌlapa (standing, moving)

Kāhea   Kumu: "Hoʻomākaukau"
            Haumāna: " ʻAe, he maʻi no ʻIolani"

He maʻi kēia ēhē āhā[1]	This is a personal chant
No ʻIolani ēhē āhā	For ʻIolani
Aia kō maʻi ēhē āhā	There is your jewel
Lā i Hiʻilawe[2] ēhē āhā	There at [the waterfall] Hiʻilawe
Ke lawe nei ēhē āhā	Your hips
Kō kīkala ēhē āhā	Are carried along
E ka lāʻau ēhē āhā	By the hard wood [the staff of the family]
Pahū a ka welo ēhē āhā	Bursting fluttering
E ka pahiolo ēhē āhā	By the saw
Ke olo nei ēhē āhā	Moving back and forth
Paʻa kō lima ēhē āhā	Clasp firmly your hands
E ʻiʻi nei ēhē āhā	Fitting tightly
Haʻina kō maʻi ēhē āhā	The personal chant has been told
Ke kuini Emalani ēhē āhā	For Queen Emma

1. A fun sound for timing and effect.
2. Highest free-fall waterfall in Hawaiʻi, on the Big Island in Waipiʻo Valley.

Nā Wahi Pana
Historic and Legendary Places

Wahi pana *refers to a place of cultural, spiritual or emotional significance. In Hawaiian thinking, a sense of place is a vital philosophical and spiritual concept. Isn't humankind a product of place, where there is a deep-rooted sense of belonging?*

My earliest pana *was Nāpoʻopoʻo, near Kealakekua Bay in Kona, Hawaiʻi island. After that it was Halehuki, Sweetheart Grandma's home in Hilo. Then it was a lovely piece of hill property at ʻĀlewa Heights, overlooking Honolulu. Great-grandpa George Langhern Desha had given the land to Mother and Papa when they were married. Papa built our Honolulu home there and there we lived while attending Kapālama English Standard School and then Kamehameha Schools. After we all graduated, Mother and Papa moved back to the Big Island. Our* pana *for our own children was Beamer Ranch in Waimea, Hawaiʻi island. Now brother Pono is our rancher and all the family members consider Beamer Ranch our family* pana. *There we strewed Papa's ashes on his favorite hillside overlooking Mauna Kea and the expanse of western sky. That is Papa's* pana, *and he continues to oversee Beamer Ranch. Yes,* pana *is the tie that binds.*

'Au'a 'Ia E Kama Ē Kona Moku
Child Hold on to Your Land

A devastating change in Hawaiian culture and lifestyle is prophesied in this chant. The composer, Keaulumoku,[1] urges Hawaiians to hold on to their land as a means of retaining some stability. We have translated this chant many times, in many different ways, and it always becomes deeper and more demanding in understanding. We thank Kahauanu Lake for permission to use this text and translation written by one of Hawai'i's most well known scholars and chanters, Ka'upena Wong.[2] His work is based on three translations of this chant done by his mentor, another of Hawai'i's famous scholars and historians, Mary Kawena Pūku'i. This *mele hula* is one of the most revered scholarly poems in the *hula* repertoire. How difficult it is to hold your emotions in check, to keep the tears from flowing out of your heart and cascading to the floor. The understanding of this text enhances the dancer's sense of pride and determination. Tears are a wellspring for a renewed commitment and belief in this treasured legacy.

Chant type: Wānana (prophetic)
Chant style: 'Aiha'a (vigorous), Ho'olaha (declarative)
Hula type: Pahu (drum), 'aiha'a (vigorous, low knee bend)

---

1. Counselor, composer and famous prophet, circa 1784.
2. From "Maiki: Aloha Mai Ka Pu'uwai, Chants & Mele of Hawaii," The Kahauanu Lake Singers, © 1992 Hula Records (#CDHS-588). Used with permission.

Kāhea
    Kumu: "Hoʻomākaukau"
    Haumāna: "'Ae, ʻauʻa ʻia e kama ē kona moku"

ʻAuʻa ʻia e kama ē kona moku	O child, look and observe thy heritage
ʻO kona moku ē kama e ʻauʻa ʻia	Thy lands, o child, retain them
ʻO ke kama, kama, kama, kama i ka hulinuʻu	Thou child, child, child, child of the highest rank
ʻO ke kama, kama, kama, kama i ka huliau	Thou child, child, child, child of the changing time
Hulihia pāpio a i lalo i ke alo	Overthrown will be the foundation, left lying face downward
Hulihia i ka imu o Kū[3] kamakiʻilohelohe[4]	Overthrown on the coral beds of Kū with the sacred cord *makiʻilohelohe*
ʻO ka hana ʻana ia hikiʻi hulahula[5]	And the cords that bound *hulahula*
Kaʻa ʻia ʻalihi aʻo pōhaku kū	Unbound are the weights that hold the land
Me ka ʻupena aku aʻo Ihuaniani[6]	Like the weights of the bonito nets of Ihuaniani
Me ka unu o Niu-olani-o-Laʻa[7]	And the temple Niu-olani-o-Laʻa
ʻO Keawe[8] ʻai kū, ʻai a Laʻahia	And from Keawe, the dedicated one
Nana i hala pepe ka honua o ka moku	He who ruled and made the island subject to him
I haʻalēʻia i ke kiu welo ka puʻu kōwelo lohi a Kanaloa[9]	His power rose to the summit of the hills, this is the powerful descendant of Kanaloa

---

3. Principal Hawaiian god of war and god of the forests.
4. Sacred cord used in *luakini* (human sacrifice) ceremonies.
5. Ceremonial killing of a pig and its offering to the gods in the *luakini* temple.
6. Probably a place or person.
7. A ruling chief of the Puna line, probably Laʻamaikahiki.
8. A chief whose full name is Keaweikekahialiʻiokamoku. He was the great-grandfather of Kamehameha the Great.
9. One of the four major Hawaiian gods; god of oceans and seas.

A Kilohana ʻO Kalani
The Chiefess Went to Kilohana

This was one of the early *hula ʻulīʻulī* (feathered-gourd rattle dances) that Sweetheart Grandma taught us. Each line ended in "lā" for rhythmic emphasis. This chant is one of a number of *mele* composed to tell the story of Queen Emma's hike to the uplands of central Kauaʻi in 1871.[1] "Upon the return of the party to Waimea, a large feast was prepared in honor of the event. All Waimea was present ... on the night of January 29.... At this feast, commemorative meles and chants, composed in honor of the trip up the mountain were recited by Kuapuu, Kaukau, Lilikalani and Kauai," wrote David Forbes.[2] The museum at Kōkeʻe State Park[3] has initiated an annual celebration honoring the queen's visit. Today's *hula* dancers gather in Kanaloahuluhulu meadow, as inspired by the *mana* (spiritual power) and beauty of this special place as were the dancers of the queen's retinue in 1871.

Chant type:	Inoa (name), Wahi Pana (place)	
Chant style:	ʻOliʻoli (joyous)	
Hula type:	ʻUlīʻulī (gourd rattle)	
Kāhea	Kumu:	"Hoʻomākaukau"
	Haumāna:	" ʻAe, a Kilohana ʻo Kalani"

A Kilohana[4] ʻo Kalani lā	The chiefess went to Kilohana
Nānā iā Hanalei lā ē	Looking towards Hanalei
ʻO ke one aʻo Mahamoku[5] lā	The sands of Mahamoku
Me ka wai aʻo Lumahaʻi[6] lā ē	And the waters of Lumahaʻi
ʻO ka lae hala ʻo Naue[7] lā	The cape of Naue with pandanus
Ālai ʻia e ka noe lā ē	Hidden by the mist

1. See also "Moe Aku," pp. 48–49. For Sweetheart Grandma's handwritten version, see Frontispiece.
2. *Queen Emma and Lawai* ([Līhuʻe], Kauaʻi: Kauaʻi Historical Society, 1970), p. 7.
3. In the Waimea district mountains at the base of the Alakaʻi bog.
4. Lookout point at 4,030 feet within Alakaʻi Swamp that overlooks Hanalei, Lumahaʻi and Wainiha Valleys on Kauaʻi's North Shore.
5. Area at mouth of Waiʻoli Stream, Hanalei.
6. Valley, stream and beach, Hanalei district.
7. Place near Hāʻena, Hanalei district, famous for pandanus trees.

I Maunahina[8] kō lalo lā	At Maunahina those below
O ke alanui kui lima lā ē	Proceed along the path hand in hand
Ui aʻe nei Emalani lā	Queen Emma asks then
E huli hoʻi kākou lā ē	Shall we all return home?
Ma ke alawai ʻōhiʻa[9] lā	Where ʻōhiʻa trees border the stream
Ala Kīpapaāola[10] lā ē	[Is the] roadway Kīpapaāola
One anakoʻo[11] ka i luna lā	[?] is above
Naele o Alakaʻi lā ē	The swamp of Alakaʻi
O kūlou a Emalani lā	As Queen Emma bows her head
I ke anu o ʻAipō[12] lā ē	In the cold of ʻAipō
Uhi paʻa mai e ka noe lā	Covered completely by the mist
Hālana mai a ka wai lā ē	Which flows towards us until reaching the water
Pūʻili lālā i ke ahi lā	Members of the group huddle around the fire
I kapa nō ia uka lā ē	A covering for the uplands
ʻO ka leo ka mea aloha lā	The voice is the beloved thing
I ka heahea ʻana mai lā ē	Calling out to us
Pehea mai ʻoukou lā	How are you all?
Ma ʻaneʻi ma ka mehana lā ē	Here in the warmth
Ka ihona o ka nahele lā	The path descends into the forest
A hiki i ka wai kai lā ē	Until it reaches the brackish waters near the sea
He piʻina ikiiki ia lā	Ascending the path is difficult
A kūkala a ka manu lā ē	Birds announce our arrival
Hoʻomaha aku ʻo Kalani lā	The chiefess rests
I ka lehua makanoe lā ē	Amidst the dwarf *lehua*
He lehua lei ʻāpiki[13] lā	A *lehua* wreath fashioned in the *piki* style
Paukū me ka paʻiniu[14] lā ē	Sectioned with the *paʻiniu*
Haʻina mai ka puana lā	Tell the refrain
Emalani nō he inoa lā ē	For Queen Emma indeed a name chant
"HE INOA NO EMALANI"	"A name chant for Queen Emma"

8. Lit., gray mountain; probably a place within Haleleʻa, a forest area, Hanalei district.
9. Flowers of the ʻōhiʻa tree, common in wet areas (*Metrosideros macropus, M. collina* subsp. *polymorpha*).
10. Lit., roadway [made] by Ola (a Kauaʻi chief); trail above Hanalei.
11. We are unsure of the meaning of "*one anakoʻo*," so we leave the translation blank. A possible substitute could be Kaʻawakō, as it matches the meaning of the *mele* at this point: lit., the ʻawa [kava] dragged along; *heiau* (temple) on the summit of Waiʻaleʻale, which, at 5,148 feet, is Kauaʻi's highest mountain.
12. Lit., eating in the dark; swamp at summit of Waiʻaleʻale.
13. Perhaps the word "*āpiki*" is used here to mean a style of *lei* that is commonly referred to as the *piki* style, which uses materials of uneven lengths, as in *lei piki* (feather garland of uneven lengths).
14. Native Hawaiian lily (*Astelia* spp.).

'Ike I Ke One Kani A'o Nohili
See the Barking Sands of Nohili

This was the first *hula 'ili'ili* (pebbles dance) we learned, though its length made it difficult for us children to memorize. The joy of gathering our own *hula* pebbles at Punalu'u black-sand beach[1] and making sure they were the right size for our hands is still a vivid childhood memory. To dance, we sat in a wide straddle position with our bodies settled firmly on the floor, the better to sway vigorously with the intent of the story. We lifted our bodies with energy and joy, which gives this *hula* type a real look of class and dedication. The *waena* (between verse) movements were always big stretches from side to side—full arms and shoulders entering into a complete lift movement, wrists and hands making a beckoning motion with each click of the pebbles. We leaned back as far as we could to do the *ka'a* (roll) with three clicks at the center-body position. Sweetheart Grandma taught us to always do the line "Ho'ohaehae" with a ritard.

We had never been to the island of Kaua'i when we learned this. Sweetheart Grandma was full of excitement about the new places we were experiencing and the stories of the Kaua'i winds and rains. We were later to travel to Hā'ena[2] to feel the *mana* (spiritual power) of the places mentioned in this chant and to pray at the *heiau* (temple) at Kē'ē.

Chant type: 'Āina (land)
Chant style: 'Oli'oli (joyous)
Hula type: 'Ili'ili (pebbles), Noho (seated)

---

1. On the southern coast of Hawai'i island, where we had one of our Desha/Beamer homes.
2. Village in the Hanalei district, northwestern Kaua'i.

Kāhea

    Kumu: "Hoʻomākaukau"
    Haumāna: " ʻAe, ʻike i ke one kani aʻo Nohili"

ʻIke i ke one kani aʻo Nohili[3]	See the barking sands of Nohili
Me ka pahapaha[4] lei aʻo Polihale[5]	With the *pahapaha* garland of Polihale
ʻIke i ka wai ʻula aʻo Mānā[6]	See the red waters of Mānā
Nā niu i hola ʻia aʻo Kaunalewa[7]	The spreading coconuts at Kaunalewa
Pā iho ka makani lā a he Kiu[8]	The Kiu wind blows
ʻIke ʻia ē ka noe lā i Niʻihau[9]	Niʻihau is shrouded in mist
Hoʻohaehae ana ē ka Nāulu[10]	Teasing by the Nāulu [wind]
Ka makani Mikiʻoi lā o Lehua[11]	The Mikiʻoi [wind] of Lehua
Pūpū-kani-oe kō Kauaʻi	Kauaʻi has land shells
Kūnihi Hāʻupu[12] ʻau i ke kai	Hāʻupu standing steep juts into the sea
Haʻina ʻia mai ana ka puana	Tell the refrain
Mokihana[13] ē ka pua la i ʻoi aʻe	The *mokihana* flower is indeed the best

"HE INOA NO KAUAʻI"   "A name chant for Kauaʻi"

---

3. Small area and point in Barking Sands, a beach in western Kauaʻi named for the sound the sands make when walked upon.
4. A sea lettuce (*Ulva* sp.).
5. State park, beach and *heiau* in the Waimea district, Kauaʻi, famous for its *pahapaha* seaweed.
6. Dry western end of Kauaʻi where Pele's sister Nāmakaokahaʻi introduced the *kaunoʻa (Cuscuta sandwichiana)*, a creeping vine belonging to the morning-glory family.
7. Area in Kauaʻi's Waimea district; a famous coconut grove was here.
8. Strong, moderately cold northwesterly wind.
9. Island just west of Kauaʻi.
10. Sea breeze at Waimea, Kauaʻi.
11. Strong, gusty wind of Lehua, a tiny island just north of Niʻihau; accompanying Pele on her first trip to Hawaiʻi, her younger sister Hiʻiaka left a *lei lehua* at this island when her brother, Kāneʻāpua, decided to stay there.
12. Peak and ridge, Līhuʻe district; probably named for a demigod.
13. Native citrus *(Pelea anisata)*; its anise-scented berry is the official "flower" of Kauaʻi.

E Hoʻi Ke Aloha I Niʻihau
Love Returns to Niʻihau

This historic chant ranks among the most worthy praise poems for Niʻihau[1] and Nihoa,[2] small islands west of Kauaʻi. It tells the story of Queen Kapiʻolani[3] admonishing her people to return to nature, thereby enriching their hearts. To this day, this chant is featured by my younger brother, Keola, at family gatherings. He and cousin Mahi Beamer developed an early appreciation for both the *hula ʻauana* (modern-style dance) and *hula kahiko* (traditional dance), being avid students of mother Louise Leiomalama. Sweetheart Grandma taught us to clap in the *waena*, the interlude between verses, with two staccato hand claps that reminded me of a stern teacher calling a class to order. The line "Aia Nihoa" was always done with a ritard.

Chant type: ʻĀina (land), Inoa (name)
Chant style: ʻOliʻoli (joyous), ʻAihaʻa (vigorous)
Hula type: Kuʻi (interpretive), ʻŌlapa (standing, moving)

Kāhea
    Kumu: "Hoʻomākaukau"   Haumāna: " ʻAe, e hoʻi ke aloha i Niʻihau"

E hoʻi ke aloha i Niʻihau ʻeā	May love return to Niʻihau
ʻO ka wai huna o ka pāoʻo[4] ʻeā	To the hidden waters of the *pāoʻo* fish
Ka ʻulu hua i ka hāpapa ʻeā	The breadfruit tree bears fruit (there) on the plains
Me ke kō ʻeli aʻo Halāliʻi[5] ʻeā	The sugar cane of Halāliʻi dug out [by hand]
Aia Nihoa ma hope ʻeā	There is Nihoa behind
ʻO ka lau hāpapa i ke kai ʻeā	With many flat reefs in the sea
ʻO ka lā welawela i ke kula ʻeā	The sun scorches the plains
Huli aku i ke alo i Kauaʻi ʻeā	Turn to face Kauaʻi
Haʻina ʻia mai ka puana ʻeā	Tell the refrain
No Kapiʻolani nō he inoa ʻeā	For Kapiʻolani indeed a name chant
"HE INOA NO KAPIʻOLANI"	"A name chant for Kapiʻolani"

1. Island in Kauaʻi County.
2. Island in the leeward Northwestern Hawaiian Islands, annexed to the Hawaiian kingdom by Kaʻahumanu in 1822.
3. Wife of King Kalākaua; granddaughter of Kaumualiʻi, the last king of an independent Kauaʻi.
4. Name for several varieties of *ʻoʻopu* (*Entomacrodus marmoratus*). This chant speaks of the fish commonly referred to as a rockskipper, which is able to leap across stretches of rocky shoreline.
5. Area with a lake in south-central Niʻihau, famed for sugar cane growing in the sand with only the leaves protruding.

He Moku Ka'ula
The Island of Ka'ula

Hearing about these small islands southwest of Kaua'i was exciting. I dearly wanted to see them, not just locate them on the map. We learned three *hula* with this chant. First was the *hula pōhaku,* which we performed with a "male" stone upright in the palm of the right hand and a "female" stone lying flat in the palm of the left hand. Second was the *hula kālā'au* (*hula* with sticks), which told the story with intriguing rhythms though the dance type itself was not particularly interesting to me. But learning the *hula 'ūlili* was a fascinating challenge. Handling the spinning gourd rattle was a new skill and oftentimes pulling the *'ūlili* string demands unladylike strength. It was not until Papa made a "smooth action" *'ūlili* for me that I really fell in love with the instrument. To this day the *hula 'ūlili* remains among my favorite *hula* types. Grandma taught this chant to us with *t*'s in place of *k*'s and *r*'s in place of *l*'s—as she had learned from her mother.

Chant type: Wahi Pana (place)
Chant style: 'Oli'oli (joyous), Mailani (sweet praise)
Hula type: Pōhaku (stones), 'Ūlili (spinning gourd rattle), Kālā'au (stick)

Kāhea
    Kumu: "Ho'omākaukau"
    Haumāna: " 'Ae, he moku Ka'ula, Nihoa me Ni'ihau"

He moku Ka'ula,[1] Nihoa[2] me Ni'ihau	The islands of Ka'ula, Nihoa and Ni'ihau are companions
I ka ulu la'i a Kawaihoa[3] a Kāne[4]	In the peaceful grove of Kawaihoa of Kāne
'O kaulana a ka lā i Halāli'i[5]	The sun shines over Halāli'i
Hala ka lā kau ma ke kua o Lehua[6]	The sun passes and rests on the back of Lehua
Kau ka mōlehulehu o ke ahiahi	The twilight of evening descends
Moe ē nō Kaua'i i luna ka lā	Asleep is Kaua'i as the sun sets
E ō ana nō Lehua i ke kai	Lehua in the sea is answering the call

1. Rocky islet southwest of Ni'ihau island.
2. A small island about a quarter square mile in area, northwest of Kaua'i and Ni'ihau. It was at one time inhabited by the ancient Hawaiians but is no longer so.
3. Lit., the companion's water; point on Ni'ihau.
4. One of the four leading Hawaiian gods, associated with sunlight, fresh water and forests.
5. Area with a lake in south-central Ni'ihau.
6. Tiny island just north of Ni'ihau.

A Puna Au
I Was in Puna

I learned about Puna[1] from happy trips with my grandparents. Grandma sang "Puna Paia 'A'ala" (Puna with Fragrant Bowers) with such sweet emotion. Now that I live there, I understand why Puna held a special place in her heart. The air is sweet with the lush growth of pandanus and *lehua,* and the myriad shades of green are soothing to the soul. The area abounds in unique Hawaiian history: the arrival of the volcano goddess Pele, the pronouncement of the Law of the Splintered Paddle by Kamehameha the Great and countless other important events. The style and poetic language of this particular *mele* indicate that it is not of the ancient or *kahiko* times but more of a contemporary piece. During my adolescent years, we sang and danced Puna songs for the Lymans, who were a prominent Puna family. Uncle Richard Lyman, former Hawai'i senator and Kamehameha Schools trustee, was the epitome of a "proper" Puna person, with quiet dignity and pride, full of love for his homeland, Puna. He and Papa were good friends. I can sing and dance about Puna now with a mature understanding. What a joy to live in Puna!

Chant type:	Wahi Pana (place)
Chant style:	'Oli'oli (joyous), Mailani (sweet praise)
Hula type:	'Ōlapa (standing, moving)

A Puna au i Kūki'i[2] au i Ha'eha'e[3]
'Ike au i ke 'ā kino lau[4] lehua

I was in Puna at Kūki'i at Ha'eha'e
I saw a supernatural *lehua* [a burning bush]

He lā'au ma lalo o ia pōhaku
Hanohano Puna e kehakeha i ka ua

A tree beneath that lava rock
Glorious Puna standing proudly in the rain

Kāhiko mau nō ia no laila
He 'āina ha'aheo loa nō Puna

It is perpetually adorned
Indeed Puna is a land cherished with great pride

I ha'aheo i ka hala me ka lehua
He maika'i ma luna he 'ā ma lalo

Grand pandanus and *lehua*
Beautiful above fiery below

He kelekele ka papa o Maukele[5]
Kāhuli 'Āpua[6] e kele ana i Maukele

Muddy is the plain of Maukele
'Āpua has been changed; steering to Maukele

"HE INOA NO PUNA HA'AHEO"

"In the name of proud Puna"

1. Lit., spring; district in southeastern Hawai'i island famous for volcanic activity and forests.
2. Lit., standing image; land division in the Maku'u area of Puna, southeast of Hilo.
3. Lit., strong affection and desire; land division near Kumukahi in the Maku'u area.
4. One of many forms taken by a supernatural being.
5. Place name at Puna; also a place in the Waipi'o Valley area, Big Island.
6. Lit., fish basket; land division and point in Puna.

APPENDIX
Chant Types and Styles
Hula Types

Chant Types

'Āina	Land
Heahea	Welcome or greeting
Ho'i	Exit
Ho'oipoipo	Romantic
Ho'okāhiko	Adorning
Ho'omaika'i	Praise, joy
Hula	Dance
Inoa	Name
Ipo	Lover
Kāhea	Calling out, request to enter
Ka'i	Entrance
Kake	Garbled
Komo	Invitation to enter
Komo Lole	Dressing
Kūō	Bombastic
Ma'i	Personal
Mōhai	Offering
Pā'ani	Play
Pule	Prayer
Wahi Pana	Place of cultural significance
Wānana	Prophetic

Chant Styles

'Aiha'a	Vigorous
Hoaaloha	Loving (friendship)
Ho'āeae	Loving (general)
Ho'oipo	Loving (personal)
Ho'oipoipo	Romantic
Ho'olaha	Declarative
Ho'onānā	Soothing, recitative
Kākala	Rough, harsh
Kānaenae	Prayerful
Kepakepa	Fast rhythmic conversation
Kūō	Bombastic
Mailani	Sweet praise
Mele Hula	Rhythmic and melodic
Olioli	Formal, nonmetered
'Oli'oli	Joyous

Hula Types

'Aiha'a	Vigorous, low knee bend
'Āla'apapa	Formal
Hoe	Paddle
Ho'i	Exit
Ho'okani	Percussion
Holo Lio	Horseback riding
Ho'onānā	Soothing, quiet
Ihe	Spear
'Ili'ili	Pebbles
Kā'eke'eke	Bamboo pipes
Ka'i	Entrance
Ka'i Hele	Processional walking entrance
Ka'i Huaka'i	Formal processional with gestures
Kake	Secretive
Kālā'au	Stick
Kānaenae	Prayerful
Kuhi Lima	Gesture
Ku'i	Interpretive
Kū I Luna	Standing up in place
Ku'i Moloka'i	Vigorous, fast-paced
Ma'i	Personal
Noho	Seated
'Ōlapa	Standing, moving
'Ōhelo	Reclining
'Ōniu	Spinning top
'O'opa	Lame
Pā'ani	Playful
Pahu	Drum
Pā Ipu	Beating the hand gourd drum
Pa'i Lima	Hand clapping
Pa'i Umauma	Chest-smiting
Pele	Volcano goddess
Pōhaku	Stones
Pū'ili	Bamboo rattle
'Ūlili	Spinning gourd [triple] rattle
'Ulī'ulī	Gourd rattle

BIBLIOGRAPHY

Beamer, Helen Desha. Private papers. Hilo, Hawai'i.

Beamer, Louise Leiomalama. 1991. Discussions of this manuscript. Puna, Hawai'i.

Beamer, Nona. 1987. *Nā Mele Hula,* vol. 1, *A Collection of Hawaiian Hula Chants.* Lā'ie, Hawai'i: Institute for Polynesian Studies.

Degener, Otto. 1973. *Plants of Hawaii National Parks: Illustrative of Plants and Customs of the South Seas.* Ann Arbor, Mich.: Braun-Brumfield. (First published in 1930)

Emerson, Nathaniel B. 1965. *Unwritten Literature of Hawai'i: The Sacred Songs of the Hula, Collected and Translated with Notes on an Account of the Hula.* Rutland, Vt.: Charles E. Tuttle Co. (First published in 1909 as Bureau of American Ethnology Bulletin 38, Washington, D.C.)

Fornander, Abraham. 1969. *An Account of the Polynesian Race, Its Origin and Migrations, and the Ancient History of the Hawaiian People to the Times of Kamehameha I.* Rutland, Vt.: Charles E. Tuttle Co. (First published in 1880, London)

Pūku'i, Mary Kawena, and Samuel H. Elbert. 1971. *Hawaiian Dictionary: Hawaiian-English, English-Hawaiian.* Honolulu: University of Hawai'i Press. (First, second and third editions of the *Hawaiian-English Dictionary* were published in 1957, 1961 and 1965, respectively; first edition of the *English-Hawaiian Dictionary* in 1964)

Pūku'i, Mary Kawena, Samuel H. Elbert and Esther T. Mo'okini. 1976. *Place Names of Hawai'i.* Revised and expanded edition. Honolulu: University of Hawai'i Press.

INDEX

'āhihi
28
'aiakahiko
10
'aiha'a (chant style)
61, 63, 66, 72
'āina (chant type)
52, 70, 72
'Aipō, Kaua'i
53, 69
'Aipō-nui, Kaua'i
48
'Akanikōlea, Hawai'i
38-39
alaka'i
5
Alaka'i, Kaua'i
69
'Ālewa, O'ahu
65
ali'i
8, 16, 27, 43, 56, 58, 61, 62-63
ali'ipoe
2, 5
aloha
7, 13, 20, 25, 28, 41, 46-47, 51, 56, 59, 60, 69, 72
altar
see *kuahu*
'ama'u
5, 48
America
60
anklets
see *kūpe'e*
Anna Ranch
50
'Āpua, Hawai'i
36, 74
'aumakua
16

Barking Sands, Kaua'i
70-71
Beamer, C. Keola (brother)
40, 61, 72
Beamer, Harriett
see Magoon
Beamer, Helen Desha
5, 7, 8, 10, 25, 26, 35, 37, 48, 54, 56, 63, 65, 68, 72-74
Beamer, Kawohi
35

Beamer, Louise Leiomalama "Dambie"
5, 61, 68, 72
Beamer, Mahi
7, 31, 40, 61, 72
Beamer, Pono (brother)
65
Beamer, Pono (father)
9-10, 65, 73
Beamer Ranch
65
beauty
25, 55, 68
Bora Bora
37
breadfruit
see *ulu*
Buck, Pearl
40

canoe
27
Carnegie Hall, New York
40
ceremony
11-21
chiefs
see *ali'i*
child
see *kama*
coconut
40, 71
cold
26, 49, 53, 57, 69
composer
7-8, 10, 52, 56, 66, 68

Desha, George Langhern
1, 2, 65
Desha, Isabella Ka'ili
1, 24, 26, 28
Desha, (Judge) Jack
56
Desha, Rev. Stephen
6, 54, 56
dressing
6-7, 23, 29-31

eel
61
Emalani Kaleleonālani
see Emma, Queen

Emerson, Nathaniel B.
18, 38
Emma, Queen
48-51, 62-63, 68-69

fern
6, 29
flower
29, 39, 53, 57, 71
forest
15-16, 18, 20, 25, 30, 48-49, 53, 55, 69
Fornander, Abraham
38
fragrance
20, 29, 30, 49

gods
13, 15, 18-19, 21
goddess
5, 13, 16, 19-21, 31, 35, 40, 74
Great Grandma
see Desha, Isabella Ka'ili

Hā'ena, Kaua'i
40-41, 70
Ha'ikamālamalama
16
Haili Church
6, 54-55
Ha'iwahine
17
hala
5, 25, 31, 47, 74
Halāli'i, Ni'ihau
72, 73
halapepe
5, 20
hālau
5
Hālauaola, Kaua'i
53
Hālawa, O'ahu
59
Halehuki
24, 26, 65
Halekauila
62
Halema'uma'u Crater, Hawai'i
35, 37, 38, 43
Hanakahi, Hawai'i
55

Hanalei, Kaua'i
48, 68-69
hapa haole
2
hau
51
Haua'iliki, Kaua'i
49, 53
Hā'upu, Kaua'i
71
Hawai'i (island)
1-2, 27, 54-55
heahea (chant type)
25
heiau
70
Hi'iaka
6, 17, 38-40
Hi'iakaikapoliopele
31, 38-39
Hi'ilawe Falls, Hawai'i
63
Hilo, Hawai'i
1-2, 27, 54-56, 65
Hina
16
hinahina
49
Hind, Mona
15, 50
hoaaloha (chant style)
25, 26
Honokāne, Hawai'i
30
Honolulu, O'ahu
62, 65
ho'oipo (chant style)
46, 56
ho'oipoipo (chant type)
46
ho'okāhiko
29, 31
ho'okupu
6, 7
ho'olaha (chant style)
24, 66
ho'omaika'i (chant type)
36, 42, 52
ho'omākaukau
3, 4, 23
ho'onānā (chant style)
31
horse
50-51, 59
hula
5, 13
hula 'aiakahiko
10
hula 'aiha'a
66
hula 'auana
2, 72

hula holo lio
50
hula ho'okani
2-3
hula ho'onānā
48
hula 'ili'ili
3, 38, 70
hula kahiko
2, 10, 72
hula ka'i
24
hula ka'i hele
17, 27, 28
hula ka'i huaka'i
18, 25, 37
hula kake
8
hula kā'lā'au
2, 3, 73
hula kuhi lima
31
hula ku'i
36, 56, 72
hula noho
4, 17, 20, 38, 48, 60, 70
hula 'ōhelo
20
hula 'ōlapa
20, 46, 50, 52, 54, 56, 61, 63, 72, 74
hula 'ōniu
40
hula pahu
52, 66
hula pa'i lima
21
hula pā ipu
3-4, 46
hula Pele
37, 42
hula pōhaku
73
hula pū'ili
4, 60
hula 'ūlili
2, 4-5, 76
hula 'ulī'ulī
4-5, 58, 68

'ie'ie
5, 16, 20
Ihuaniani
67
'ili'ili
2, 3; see also *hula 'ili'ili*
'ilima
57
inoa (chant type)
18, 38, 48, 50, 56, 58, 60, 68, 72
instrumentation
2

Inuwai
31
'Iolani
see Kamehameha IV
ipu
2, 3

Johnson, Rubellite Kawena
61

Ka'aihue, Marmionette
7
Kaeppler, Adrienne
52
Kahale'iole'ole
2
Kahanu, Princess Elizabeth
1, 56
Kaha'ula
21
kāhea (chant type)
24
Kahiki
19, 37, 42-43
Kaho'ānokū
61
kāhuli
8
kahuna pule
15
ka'i (chant type)
24, 27, 28, 36, 37
ka'i hele (chant type)
15
Kaipalaoa, Hawai'i
2
Kaipuha'a, Kaua'i
24
Kaiwiku'i
41
Kaka'ako Mission School
8
kākala (chant style)
2
kake
8
kālā'au
3
Kalākaua, King David
52, 53
Kalaniana'ole, Prince Jonah Kūhiō
56
Kaliuwa'a, O'ahu
38
kama
66-67
Kamahu'alele
27
kāmakahala
28
Kamapua'a
38

Kameali'i
    see Kaumealani
Kamehameha I
    2, 47, 61, 74
Kamehameha II
    46-47
Kamehameha IV
    62-63
Kamehameha Schools
    10, 48, 56, 65
Kamuela, Hawai'i
    65
kānaenae (chant style)
    15-18, 20, 21, 36
Kanaloa
    41, 67
Kanaloahuluhulu, Kaua'i
    68
Kāne
    17, 18, 37
Kānehoa, O'ahu
    29
kapa
    16
Kapa'a, Kaua'i
    24
Kapālama, O'ahu
    65
Kapela
    52
Kapi'olani, Queen
    54-55, 72
Kapo
    15
kapu
    46
Kapuailohiamanonokalani
    46
Kaua'i
    24, 38, 48, 70-73
Kauaikanānā, Kaua'i
    49
Kaukeano, O'ahu
    51
Ka'ula
    31, 53, 73
Kaumealani
    52
Kaunā, Hawai'i
    36
Kaunalewa
    71
kauna'oa
    see *kauno'a*
kauno'a
    8
Kawaiaha'o Church
    56
Kawaihoa, Ni'ihau
    73
Kawaikapu
    30

Kawaikini
    24
Kealakekua Bay, Hawai'i
    65
Keaulumoku
    66
Keawe
    67
Kē'ē, Kaua'i
    70
Kekuaokalani
    46
ki'i pā
    2-5, 20
kīkepa
    30
Kīlauea, Hawai'i
    31, 35, 37, 55
Kilohana, Kaua'i
    48, 68
kilu
    40
Kīna'u (horse)
    50-51
Kinoiki, Princess
    56-57
kino lau
    16, 21, 74
Kīpapaāola, Kaua'i
    69
Kiu
    71
Kiuke'e
    57
kō
    72
koa
    28, 56
Kōke'e, Kaua'i
    53, 68
komo (chant style)
    26
komo lole (chant type)
    30
Kona
    26, 46, 65
Kū
    67
kuahu
    5, 13, 15-17, 20
Kuamo'o, Hawai'i
    46
Kūhiō, Prince
    see Kalaniana'ole
Kūki'i, Hawai'i
    74
kukui
    57
Kūlili
    36
kumu hula
    6, 7, 13, 15, 18

kūō (chant style)
    42
kūō (chant type)
    54
kūpe'e
    5-6, 23, 29
Kupehau, Hawai'i
    30
kūpuna
    1, 2

la'amia
    5
Laka
    5, 13-21
Lake, Kahauanu
    66
lama
    5, 16
Lāna'i
    8
land shells
    48, 71
laua'e
    20
lau hala
    5
Law of the Splintered Paddle
    2, 74
ledger
    9, 10, 49, 50, 54, 62-63
Lehua (island)
    53, 71, 73
lehua
    20, 25, 28, 29, 36, 55, 69, 74
lehua maka noe
    53, 69
lei
    5-7, 16, 17, 23, 29, 31, 38, 54-55,
    69, 71
Leilehua, O'ahu
    59
Liholiho
    see Kamehameha II
Līhu'e, O'ahu
    29
Lili'uokalani, Queen
    58-59
Limahuli, Kaua'i
    41
Lohi'au
    38, 40-41
Lono
    19
love
    see *aloha*
Luahine, 'Iolani
    26, 42, 63
Lualualei, O'ahu
    28
lū'au
    7, 68; see also Queen's Surf Lū'au

Lumaha'i, Kaua'i
68
Lunalilo, King William Charles
60
Lyman, Richard
74

Magoon, Harriett Beamer
35, 42
Mahamoku, Kaua'i
68
ma'i (chant type)
61, 63
mailani (chant style)
28-30, 36-38, 48, 50, 52, 54, 60, 73, 74
maile
16, 21
Maka'ike'ole, Kaua'i
53
Mākālei
19
Makana, Kaua'i
41
maki'ilohelohe
67
Malama, Hawai'i
39
Māluakele
53
mana
5, 19, 68, 70
Mānā, Kaua'i
71
Mānana, O'ahu
59
Mānoa, O'ahu
53
Manono, Chiefess
46-47
Maukele, Hawai'i
55
Mauna'ala, O'ahu
56
Maunahina, Kaua'i
69
Mauna Kea, Hawai'i
55, 65
Maunalahilahi, O'ahu
28
Maunaloa, Moloka'i
20
mele
1
mele hula
1, 2, 33
mele inoa
7-8; see also *inoa*
mele ma'i
8, 61, 63
mele oli
18, 23

mele poo
10
melody
8, 10, 50, 60, 62
Miki'oi
71
mist
15-16, 18, 25, 37, 53, 55, 68-69, 71
Moanalua, O'ahu
59
Mō'īkeha
27
Mōkaulele, Hawai'i
55
mokihana
53, 71
Moloka'i
2
Mo'oheau Park, Hawai'i
56
Mo'ohela'ia, Hawai'i
20
mountain
16, 18, 24, 30

Nākoa, Sarah
61
Nāpo'opo'o, Hawai'i
65
Naue, Kaua'i
31, 68
Nāulu
71
Nihoa
72, 73
Ni'ihau
31, 71-73
Nishimitsu, Pōhaku
8, 52
Niu-olani-o-La'a
67
Nohili, Kaua'i
70, 71
Nounou, Kaua'i
24
Nu'uanu, O'ahu
28, 56

O'ahu
28, 65
ohelo
49
'ōhi'a kū
20
'ōhi'a lehua
5, 69
oli
1
oli komo
26
oli kūpe'e
29

oli lei
31
'oli'oli (chant style)
27, 40, 50, 56, 58, 68, 70, 72-74
olioli (chant style)
28, 31
oli pā'ū
30
'ōniu
40

pa'ani (chant type)
40
pahapaha
71
pahu
2, 41
Pā'ie'ie, Hawai'i
55
pa'iniu
48, 69
pā 'ipu
see *hula pā ipu*
pala'ā
20
palapalai
5, 17, 20
Pana'ewa, Hawai'i
10, 36
pao'o
72
Papaakanēnē, Hawai'i
36
Papa'i Bay, Hawai'i
2
Papalauahi, Hawai'i
39
pā'ū
23, 30, 50; *pā'ū heihei* 6; *pā'ū kī/lā'ī/lau kī* 6, 19, 30, 35, 37
Pele
31, 35-43, 74
Perry, Anna Fiske
50
plains
27, 36, 55, 57, 59, 72
Poire, Nāpua Stevens
x
Polapola
see Bora Bora
Poli'ahu, Kaua'i
57
Polihale, Kaua'i
71
prayer
18; see also *pule*
protocol
5-6, 23
pū'ili
see *hula pū'ili*
Pūku'i, Mary Kawena
8, 52, 66

Puʻuhinahina, Kauaʻi
    41
Puʻukāhea
    26
Puʻulena
    55
Puʻuʻoniʻoni, Hawaiʻi
    38-39
Puʻuwaʻawaʻa, Hawaiʻi
    50
pule (chant type)
    15-17, 20, 21, 36
Puna, Hawaiʻi
    2, 31, 39, 57, 74
Punaluʻu, Hawaiʻi
    70
pūpū-kani-oe
    see land shells

Queen's Surf Lūʻau
    15, 18

rain
    30, 36, 53, 74; Waʻahila 53
rainbow
    15
religion/Christianity
    6, 16, 46
respect
    2, 5, 6, 42-43, 61
rhythm
    3-5, 73
ritual
    5-7, 11-21

salt
    6
sea
    16, 31, 36, 57, 60, 69, 71-73
ship
    60
Silva, Kalena
    10
sitting *hula*
    see *hula noho*
songs
    7, 8, 38, 56

Spencer, Johnny
    8
sugar cane
    see *kō*
sun
    36, 51, 53, 72, 73
Sweetheart Grandma
    see Beamer, Helen Desha

Tahiti
    27
tapa
    see *kapa*
Tatar, Elizabeth
    1, 52
teaching
    7-8, 13
temples
    see *heiau*
ti
    5
ti-leaf skirt
    see *pāʻū kī/lāʻī/lau kī*
train
    58-59
translation
    8, 52, 61, 66

Uēhanokahuna, Hawaiʻi
    55
ʻūlili
    see *hula ʻūlili*
ʻulīʻulī
    see *hula ʻulīʻulī*
ulu
    72
uluhe
    5, 13, 46, 47
Unulau, Hawaiʻi
    10, 36
Unulau (wind)
    53

vamp
    2
volcano
    35, 74

Waʻahila, Oʻahu
    53
waena
    2-3, 70, 72
Wahiawā, Oʻahu
    29
Wahinekapu, Hawaiʻi
    39
Wahinekapu, Kauaʻi
    55
wahi pana
    65; (chant type) 24, 27, 28, 68, 73, 74
Waiʻaleʻale, Kauaʻi
    24, 52-53
Waiʻanae, Oʻahu
    28
Waiau, Henry
    8
Waikōloa
    29
Wailua, Kauaʻi
    24, 57
Waimea, Hawaiʻi
    50, 65
Waimea, Kauaʻi
    68, 71
Waineki, Kauaʻi
    48
Waiʻōpua
    41
Waipiʻo, Hawaiʻi
    2, 30, 63
wānana (chant type)
    66
water
    17, 57, 68-69, 71, 72
Wāwaenohu, Kauaʻi
    53
wind
    29, 37, 53; Inuwai 31; Kiu 71; Kiukeʻe 57;
    Māluakele 53; Mikiʻoi 71; Nāulu 71;
    Puʻulena 55; Unulau 53; Waikōloa 29;
    Waiʻōpua 41
Wong, Kaʻupena
    8, 15, 52, 66
wristlets
    see *kūpeʻe*

INDEX TO FIRST LINES

'A'ala kupukupu i ka uka o Kāneboa 29
Aia i Haili kō lei nani 55
A ka luna o Pu'u'oni'oni 39
A ke kuahiwi i ke kualono 18
A Kilohana 'o Kalani lā 68
Aloha nā hale o mākou 26
A Puna au i Kūki'i au i Ha'eha'e 74
'Au'a 'ia e kama ē kona moku 67
E hea i ke kanaka 26
E ho'i ke aloha i Ni'ihau 'eā 72
Eia au e Laka 17
Eia Hawai'i he moku he kanaka 27
E Manono lā 'eā 47
E nā kānaka 2
Hālau Wai'anae molale i ka lā 28
He ma'i kēia ēhē āhā 63
He ma'i no Kalani ha'uha'u ē 61
He moku Ka'ula, Nihoa me Ni'ihau 73
He wahine holo lio 'oe ā 51
Ho'opuka ē ka lā i kai o Unulau 36

I aloha i kō a ka wai lā 57
'Ike i ke one kani a'o Nohili 71
Kākua pā'ū 'ahu nā kīkepa 30
Kau lī lua i ke anu Wai'ale'ale 53
Kēia 'ala o ka pā'ū kī 30
Ke lei maila 'o Ka'ula i ke kai 31
Ke pohā nei 'u'ina lā 41
Kūnihi ka mauna i ka la'i ē 24
Lapakū ka wahine a'o Pele i Kahiki 43
Mai Kahiki ka wahine 'o Pele 37
Ma kai a'o Halekauila lā 62
Moe aku i ka hale 'ama'u 48
Noho ana ke akua i ka nāhelehele 15
Noho ana 'o Laka i ka uluwehiwehi 20
No ke ano ahiahi ke aloha lā 60
'O Laka ke ali'i o nu'u 16
'O Lanakila ke ka'aahi ali'i 59
Onaona i ka hala me ka lehua 25
Pūpū weuweu e Laka ē 21